Praise for *Favor*

"*Favor* combines historical research with inventive theatricality to explore the intersection of art, politics, and moral account-ability. This gripping, timely, trenchant play challenges audiences to confront the complexities of personal obligation in the face of societal collapse."
—Tyler Dobrowski, Artistic Director at Philadelphia Theatre Company

"What an exciting challenge for actors and directors who want to engage with a playwright who combines deep historical research with a compellingly inventive theatrical imagination! Damkoehler's play breathes life into a nearly forgotten musical genre, and recreates an historical moment in which entertain-ment, politics, misinformation, and self-delusion form a massive web of permission for the denial of personal responsibility. The play barrels forward and backwards in time, yet maintains relent-less forward motion as its real-life protagonist sinks deeper and deeper into a self-created cesspool of moral rot. With theatri-cal flair and deep psychological insight, *Favor* bores relentlessly into the soul of an artist who refuses to acknowledge the hideous price of his neutrality. It could not be more timely or more act-able. This is a play that really needs to be read . . . and produced."
—Brian McEleney, professional actor, director, playwright,
    Founding Director, Brown University/Trinity Rep M. F. A.
    Acting Program

"Bill Damkoehler is a great man of the theatre—a fantastic actor, director and playwright. I have been blessed in my career to act

alongside Bill, to be directed by him and to have been cast in workshops of his plays. His play *Favor* is fascinating and well-timed, as our world seems more and more to repeat the mistakes of the past rather than progress to the future. The question of separating an artist's work from the times in which he lives resonates today as profoundly as in earlier troubled times. *Favor* is different in tone than any of Bill's other plays, which is beyond impressive; it's simply world class, and demands your attention."
—Fred Sullivan, Jr., professional actor, director, theater educator

"I am wowed by William Damkoehler's new play, *Favor*—a brilliantly-crafted, two act play within a play; a fugue-infused work of creative genius and the utter embodiment of avant-garde theatre."
—Fred Rosenblum, left coast poet

Praise For *Self Storage and The Occupant*
(Also available from Fomite Press)

"William Damkoehler's witty, and oft times ferociously funny, duet—*Self Storage and The Occupant*, reveals to the discerning eye a seasoned dramatist's attention to detail and a strict focus for converting a native ear, evolved and trained, to veritably 'talk the talk' in these two flawless bodies of work—both contemporary gems of genuine human dialogue ..."
—Fred Rosenblum, bawdy American poet whose latest collection is entitled *Tramping Solo*

"With humor, mystery, and a touch of pathos, *Self Storage* is a trim, ninety-minute play featuring four wonderfully rich roles

for veteran actors. Easy to produce, and a pleasure to perform, it spins a funny, rich story from one of the most quotidian-yet-tantalizing riddles in modern society: what the heck is in that guy's storage container?"
—Tyler Dobrowski, Artistic Director at Philadelphia Theatre Company

"William Damkoehler miraculously uncovers worlds of complexity in the unlikely setting of a humble storage unit. With nods to Beckett, Shakespeare, Chaplin and Groucho Marx, he manages to infuse his eminently actable dialogue with a playfulness that poses deep existential questions. As his characters struggle with issues of life, death, loss and bewilderment, they find wonder and relief in moments of transcendence that echo centuries of theatrical magic. As a playwright, Damkoehler understands that every one of us keeps a protected self under lock and key; and as a life-long theatre artist he understands that it is often through the power of art, magic, and imagination that we are able, for a moment at least, to raise the metal door that protects our fragile inner lives. *Self Storage* is a miracle of artful simplicity—I can't imagine a mature actor who wouldn't be thrilled to play any one of these roles."
—Brian McEleney, professional actor, director, playwright, Founding Director, Brown University/Trinity Rep M.F.A. Acting Program

"I just love *Self Storage*! Bill's play is theatrical, smart, funny— and trust me: you don't know where it's going."
—Phyllis Kay, professional actor

"Within these two plays, we find deeply flawed characters hellbent on creating situations that are both hilarious and heart-warming. Through their underlying stories, we dip our toes into vital drama which feels timely and important to our current culture. Bravo to Bill Damkoehler for sharing this thoroughly entertaining work with us."
—Kate Porter, author, *Lessons In Disguise*

"I have loved Bill Damkoehler as an actor, director, and human being for forty years, and now know him as a really special play-wright. *Self Storage* is simply remarkable—surprising, magic, and indelibly human. This play has everything for a wonderful night of theater. Bill is a great man of the theater and I applaud him once again!"
—Fred Sullivan, Jr., professional actor, director, theater educator

FAVOR

**A play with music
Inspired by a true story**

**by
William Damkoehler**

Fomite
Burlington, VT

For questions about producing, or about any other aspect of this play, please contact the author through his website: www.billdam.com

ISBN-13: 978-1-967022-11-3
Library of Congress Control Number: 2025948499
Fomite
58 Peru Street
Burlington, VT 05401

11-18-2025

For Cym—my muse, critic, humor savant, and exuberant co-conspirator in art and life…

Contents

Introduction

Early in the year 1905, the Viennese librettist Leo Stein came across an old comic play whose plot revolved around a marriage scheme designed to employ the fortune of a wealthy widow as support for the economy of a failing duchy. Mr. Stein thought the farce well-suited for adaptation as an operetta and engaged a composer to provide a score. But unsatisfied with the result, Stein turned to the Austro-Hungarian composer famous for his operettas, Franz Lehár, who accepted the work and developed a sublime score within a matter of months. *Die Lustige Witwe* (*The Merry Widow*) opened in Vienna on December 30, 1905, ran for 483 performances there, and went on to become one of the most enduring operettas ever created — estimated to have been performed half a million times in its first 60 years alone, and still performed in many languages to this day.

Thousands of those half-million performances featured a Dutch immigrant to Germany, who played the role of Count Danilo in productions of *The Merry Widow* across a span of 30 years — years that witnessed the rise and fall of the Third Reich. This actor/singer/dancer was Johannes Heesters, who became Adolf Hitler's favorite actor, and who performed actively on stage, television, and in the German film industry well into the 21st century, until shortly before his death in 2011 at the age of 108. At the age of 98 — like Hansel Hals, the main character in *Favor* — Heesters played the role of the aging manservant Firs in a production of Chekhov's *The Cherry Orchard*, another historical fact that gives structure to my play.

But *Favor* is not documentary. Many events in the play actually occurred, but they are not necessarily presented in the play in historically accurate chronological order. And, again, Hansel Hals is a fictional character, as are most other characters in the play (besides the obvious ones, who will be recognized more as caricature than character). But the fictional Hansel Hals, as well as some of his fictional colleagues, is trapped by a real-world dilemma: what is the duty of a high profile public figure, a recognized artist, under an oppressive political system? Private citizens in the play, as in real life, face the same dilemma. And what motivates their ultimate choices? Political ideology? Religion? Personal philosophy? Or desire for recognition, career advancement, favor . . .?

Lines from Chekhov's *The Cherry Orchard* used in this play are taken from the Public Domain translation found on the "Project Gutenberg" website. The lines and scenes employed here are not necessarily in the same order as in Chekhov's script and the lines may not always be in the mouth of the character to whom Chekhov assigned them. Lines from *The Sound Of Music* are not direct quotes but are paraphrased to convey the gist. Music from *The Merry Widow* is as written by Franz Lehár, but some of the lyrics have been altered. The lyrics that remain unaltered are the original 1907 English translation which is, as is Lehár's music, in the Public Domain. All other music and lyrics are traditional, Public Domain, or original with me. Sheet music is in the Appendix. Most of the German language in the script is based on Google translation service and should be vetted by a reliable German-speaker before production.

Favor has received several staged readings, or "Readers Theater" treatments, and was very warmly received. The text of the play contains stage directions that are meant to not only guide a full staging, but also to be read aloud and provide context and forward momentum in a Readers Theater environment.

And for those who enjoy reading plays in order to fully produce them if only in the Theater Of The Mind, your curtain rises when you turn this page…

"Choices are the hinges of destiny."
—Pythagoras

FAVOR

CAST OF CHARACTERS:

HANSEL HALS: An entertainer—that is, an actor/singer/dancer. He is handsome, athletic. He can appear to be any age from 25 to 105, 110, 115, or more!

FREDERIKA ("FRIKA") HALS: Hansel's sister. Plain, simple, passionate. She can appear to be between 20 and 35 years old.

SILKE SONNTAG: A film star. Movie-star beautiful. She also sings and dances. She can appear to be between 25 and 40 years old.

FRANZ LUFT: An A-list German film director.

GERHART: An actor.

OSCAR: An actor. (played by the same actor who plays Franz)

BUREAUCRAT OF THE REALM: A government official; then a military officer. (played by the same actor who plays Gerhart)

LOPAKHIN: Character in "The Cherry Orchard." (played by the same actor who plays Gerhart)

GAEV: Character in "The Cherry Orchard." (played by the same actor who plays Franz)

DUNYASHA: Character in "The Cherry Orchard." (played by the same actor who plays Frika)

ANYA: Character in "The Cherry Orchard." (played by the same actor who plays Frika)

FIRS: Character in "The Cherry Orchard." (played by the same actor who plays Hansel)

LUBOV: Character in "The Cherry Orchard." (played by the same actor who plays Silke)

ADOLPH HITLER: Historical figure. (played by the same actor who plays Franz)

LENI RIEFENSTAHL: Historical figure. (played by the same actor who plays Silke)

SS GUARDS: Three German SS Troopers. (played by the same actors who play Franz, Silke and Frika)

LAUTSPRECHER: Voice from a loudspeaker/monitor. (some live, some recorded)

NOTE ON CASTING:
This play can be produced with a minimum of five actors.

NOTE ON MUSIC:
Musical accompaniment can be provided by one piano and a piano player somewhere on set, plus incidental recorded music.

SCENE:
Berlin and elsewhere.

TIME:
Late 1920s thru Present

ACT I
Scene 1

*The **OVERTURE** (the famous waltz from Franz Lehár's "**THE MERRY WIDOW**") ends. The **MUSICAL INTRO** into the opening number begins. LIGHTS reveal what is apparently an all-purpose movie set from the 1920s. Lighting instruments on wheels are scattered about, as are scenery flats, a sofa and other pieces of furniture, fat electrical cords, etcetera. Posted on walls here and there are many movie posters, most bearing the image of HANSEL HALS. Some posters bear the image of SILKE SONNTAG. Still other posters show HANSEL and SILKE together, proclaiming "HALS UND SONNTAG!" All the posters are written in German. An introductory vamp to the opening number continues, urgently, as HANSEL HALS, an actor, sits at a typical dressing room mirror. Seated nearby is another actor, GERHART. THEY are both attending to details of their makeup. The **MUSICAL VAMP** continues, even more urgently, an obvious cue for someone to begin singing a song—RIGHT NOW! HANSEL takes a last look at himself in the mirror then pivots to look at the audience. HE wears a black and white costume that lends him the air of a bon vivant on the town, or perhaps a maitre d', or maybe even a butler, manservant, or footman—yes, maybe a footman—and HE appears to be very, very old—perhaps 100, 105, 110—OLD! But his innate performer's enthusiasm is unquenchable...*

HANSEL
Yes, yes, all right ... if you insist!

HE rises stiffly from his dressing chair and approaches center stage.

HANSEL (cont'd)
My trademark song, from "The Merry Widow"...

*HE clears his throat as the **VAMP** continues.*

HANSEL (cont'd)
...which I gladly sing for you ... for the fifty thousandth time!
I'm delighted, of course; and thank you for your everlastingly
generous—

*The **MUSICAL VAMP** absolutely DEMANDS that HE
begin the number!*

HANSEL (cont'd)
Yes! Yes, as you wish.

*HE executes a small bow, then begins to sing, directly to
the audience, the last few verses of "**MAXIM'S**," Count
Danilo's entrance number from the operetta "**THE
MERRY WIDOW**." HE sings with a voice that's a bit
rough around the edges, for he is, after all, over 100 years-
old... Nevertheless, energetically striving to entertain, HE
sparkles for a while with the glow of a born entertainer.
HE seems light and carefree.*

HANSEL (cont'd)
I GO OFF TO MAXIM'S
WHERE FUN AND FROLIC BEAMS!

WITH ALL THE GIRLS I CHATTER,
I LAUGH AND KISS AND FLATTER!

LOLO, DODO, JOU-JOU,
CLO-CLO, MARGOT, FROU-FROU,

FOR SURNAMES DO NOT MATTER
I TAKE THE FIRST TO HAND!

AND THEN THE CORKS GO POP!
WE DANCE AND NEVER STOP!

THE LADIES SMILE SO SWEETLY,
I CATCH AND KISS THEM NEATLY!

LOLO, DODO, JOU-JOU,
CLO-CLO, MARGOT, FROU-FROU

TILL I FORGET COMPLETELY—

> *HE breaks off, coughs a bit, the* **MUSIC** *falters then
> ceases. A smattering of offstage applause can be heard,
> as if coming from the loudspeaker of a theater backstage
> monitor system. HANSEL waves off the applause...*

HANSEL (cont'd)
Thank you. Thank you. But, no, please. That will do...
    (The applause trickles off...)
I must save myself for...
    (Gestures over his shoulder)
for the ... play.

> *From the loudspeaker comes the quiet sound of VOICES
> in dialogue from a play. Occasional words stand out,
> such as "peasant," and "money," and "sell," and, definitely,
> "cherry orchard."*

HANSEL (cont'd)
Yes... Chekhov!
    (Referring to the overheard dialogue)
You recognize the dialogue? Of course you do, my smart, loyal
admirers; so dear to me! So dear... Chekhov's "The Cherry
Orchard." In what other play is there a role for an actor my age?
Over one hundred years old! *Mehr als einhundert Jahre!* That's
me! Eight performances a week! Six days a week! *And I still got*

it! Show me any actor else who can do what I can do! You can't! But, I must save it, you know, for my ...

(Gestures over his shoulder)

my "comeback" engagement. You will excuse me, please...

HANSEL crosses to a microphone standing somewhere among the wires and cables, steps up to it, clears his throat, and as the "LAUTSPRECHER," makes an announcement. HANSEL's voice booms from the loudspeaker:

LAUTSPRECHER

In A Theater Dressing Room, Somewhere In Germany, Hansel Hals,
(HE can't help but indicate his famous self)
The Ancient Dutch Actor Once Famous Throughout Europe,
(Again, HE proudly indicates himself)
Prepares For His First Entrance On A Fateful Opening Night!

HANSEL returns to the makeup table, sits. HE and GERHART both tend to details of hair, or makeup, or costume as they converse. Soft snippets of dialogue continue from the monitor. GERHART occasionally checks a cell phone...

GERHART

My grandfather told me last night he'd seen you perform, many years ago. "The Merry Widow."

HANSEL

My great triumph! Where? Germany? Austria?

GERHART

Berlin. West Berlin.

HANSEL

My trademark operetta role: Count Danilo. Performed it thousands of times. Always to great acclaim. Great acclaim!

GERHART

Well, he loved you. And all your films. Including the silents.

HANSEL

I was very well-loved. Had tens of thousands of admirers. Your great-grandfather—he loved me, too, yes? And your great-great-grandfather? Yes? Your great-great-great-great—

GERHART

Maybe!

HANSEL

"Maybe?" "Maybe," you say? Of course they loved me!

> *The actor playing the role of FRIKA has stepped up to the microphone. SHE makes a LAUTSPRECHER announcement, as the Stage Manager:*

LAUTSPRECHER

Ladies and gentleman of the cast and crew, a quick reminder—forgot to mention at half-hour: Cherry Orchard opening night party right after the show tonight. In the lobby. Open bar. Spread the word. Thank you...

> *Snippets of dialogue again are heard over the monitor, then...*

GERHART

Coming to the party?

HANSEL

I never miss a party with an open bar.

> *GERHART laughs.*

HANSEL (cont'd)

And at my age, who knows? One's next party might be one's
last party.

GERHART laughs.

HANSEL (cont'd)

I'm over one hundred, you know.

GERHART

Yes, I know. Amazing!

HANSEL

I won't say how much over. I'm allowed my secrets.

GERHART

Then I won't ask!

HANSEL

I could take you in a contest of arm-wrestling.

GERHART

Sorry...? What...?

HANSEL

(Absolutely serious)
Arm-wrestling. I could overcome you. Easily.

GERHART

I ... won't ... rise to that challenge, Hansel!

HANSEL

Your grandfather... German?

GERHART

Yes. Well, Austrian.

HANSEL

Mm.

GERHART

Austrian-Polish, I think.

HANSEL

Mm hm.
(Quietly sings a little snippet of "**EDELWEISS**" from
"**THE SOUND OF MUSIC**")
"EDELWEISS, EDELWEISS, DU GRUSST MICH JEDEN MOR-GEN..."

GERHART

(Chuckles...)
The Hills Are Alive...

HANSEL

(Laughs...)
Yes! Yes!
(More serious)
Oh, boy, why do I laugh? That show caused me some trouble.

GERHART

Oh. Right.

HANSEL

Some trouble...

GERHART

The Sound Of Mu—

HANSEL

The Sound Of Disaster. Career-ending disaster. They killed me.
Idiot producers! Stupid! I don't wish to talk about it...

HANSEL and GERHART listen for a moment to the
ongoing dialogue coming from the monitor; then:

HANSEL (cont'd)

I am Dutch.

GERHART

Ah. I know.

HANSEL

Made my Dutch name famous throughout Germany. All of
Europe.

GERHART

Mmm...

HANSEL

Had hundreds of thousands of admirers...
          (Points toward the monitor speaker)
Are you listening? No laughs. It's like they are in church out
there. A graveyard. Chekhov is comedy! It's obvious! But who
listens to me? Speaking of— Gerhart, you are missing a chance
for a good laugh. In the scene with the maid.

GERHART

Oh?

HANSEL

Yes, yes. Let me instruct you: When she tells you she has had a
proposal of marriage, you should—after you respond "Ah?"—
you should then roll your eyes. Play it out. Yes? Such as this...

HANSEL turns out toward the audience and
demonstrates his idea by rolling his head and his eyes in
a hugely exaggerated expression of amusement that the
maid should be worthy of a marriage proposal.

HANSEL (cont'd)

You see? Like so...
> *HE demonstrates the action again.*

HANSEL (cont'd)

Now you do it. Show me.

GERHART

Well ... I'd rather ...
> (Trying to joke)

Union regulations, you know: Play it as directed!

HANSEL

Ach. She is no director. Only she is a traffic policeman. *"Go here. Go there. Stage right. Stage left. Sit here. Stand there..."* I worked with directors! Men of character. With vision! Ideas!

GERHART

Mmm...

> *GERHART rises a bit from his seat, leans toward the mirror and last-minute checks his makeup, his hair, as he prepares to leave.*

GERHART (cont'd)

With Franz Luft, right?

HANSEL

Yes, Luft! All the great ones! Murnau! Pabst! Others... The entertainment films.

GERHART

For the Third—

> *GERHART stops speaking abruptly.*

HANSEL

Entertainment films! Yes! Say it! For the Third Reich! Why not?
My films distracted countless people during war! People forget:
That was a very difficult time, let me tell you—

GERHART rises fully from his place at the dressing table.

GERHART

Hold that thought, Hansel—that's my cue.

HANSEL

Yes. Of course. Merde.

GERHART

Thanks.

*GERHART leaves the dressing room. HANSEL listens a
bit more to the disembodied dialogue from the monitor;
then...*

HANSEL

"Hold that thought, Hansel..."

*HE gets up stiffly from his chair, faces the audience;
although well over a hundred years-old, HE speaks with
defiant vigor:*

HANSEL (cont'd)

"Hold that thought, Hansel..." "Hold that thought, Hansel!"
No. You hold *this* thought: It was war! It was world war! So,
what did I do wrong? Nothing! They were entertainment
films! Not propaganda! To distract my audiences! Was that a
crime? For a talent such as mine, was that a crime? No! And
the Allies agreed, after the war. They allowed me to continue
to work. For my *people*! And sure, I wanted to make a career!
Why should I not?

(HE strides to the microphone, speaking as he crosses)
Talent must out!

*HE reaches the microphone, speaks into it; his voice blasts
from the loudspeaker:*

LAUTSPRECHER
*Hansel Hals Recalls A Much, Much, MUCH Earlier Time! Of
Course, Ancient As He Is, His Memory May Not Be Entirely
Reliable...*

RECORDED MOVIE MUSIC *(See PRODUCTION
NOTES at end of play*) begins: solo piano playing a
minimal arrangement of "**THE MERRY WIDOW
WALTZ.**"*

*Meanwhile, the LIGHTS change; they are flickering in
strobe-like fashion, creating the illusion of movie action.*

*HANSEL is re-adjusting his costume as HE shouts into
the wings:*

HANSEL
Frika! We're on! Let's show these Germans The Best Of Dutch
Vaudeville!

*HANSEL speaks again into the microphone; his voice
booms again:*

LAUTSPRECHER
*Screen Test, Merry Widow Ballroom Dance Sequence: Hals And
Hals! Take One!*

*FREDERIKA "FRIKA" HALS, HANSEL's sister, wearing
an elegant ball gown, sweeps onto the set and dances over
to HANSEL, who now seems to be dressed in an elegant*

13

tuxedo, and looks 20-years-old. HANSEL joins FRIKA in the dance, which soon becomes very intimate, sensual, ending in a passionate embrace, leading to an inevitable kiss. But at the decisive moment, both HANSEL and FRIKA burst out laughing! THEY appear to be embarrassed by the idea of kissing each other. The **MUSIC** *growls to a halt, the flickering of the lights ends. The "Screen Test" is over. A megaphone-enhanced voice booms from somewhere in the audience. It is the voice of FRANZ LUFT, a film director:*

FRANZ
(From the audience)
What? What's the joke?

HANSEL and FRIKA laugh again, mightily embarrassed.

FRANZ
(Making his way to the stage)
You're amused? You just wasted very expensive film stock, you know. And a quarter hour of my time. What comedy am I missing here?

FRANZ has reached the stage. HE continues across to the microphone.

FRIKA
I'm sorry—

HANSEL
Let us go again.

FRANZ
Absolutely not.
(HE drops the megaphone, shouts into the microphone; his voice blasts from the loudspeaker)
Silke Sonntag! To the sound stage! In costume! NOW!

14

(Turns to HANSEL and FRIKA)

I knew this was a bad idea. *"A Brother/Sister act from Holland! Oh, you will love them, Franz! They are so talented! He sings! They dance! The Best Of Dutch Vaudeville!"* The best of Dutch Vaudeville…? That's like saying, the … the best of … English Cuisine.

FRIKA

Please, Herr Luft, it's my fault. To kiss my brother … that way… for the camera. I was too embarrassed, but, I—

FRANZ

Well, of course you were embarrassed, dear. You haven't lost your sense of decency—unlike the rest of us in this incestuous hellhole of a city. How refreshing! But, who knows? Maybe these good Germans would pay to see a brother and sister as lovers onscreen. Hmm? Give themselves a *verboten* pornographic thrill?

FRIKA

Then you will let me try again?

FRANZ

Oh, God in heaven, no! You misunderstand. You can sing, though, correct? As well as dance?

HANSEL

My sister has many talents.

FRANZ

(To Frika)

What is your name? "Frederika?"

FRIKA

Frik—

HANSEL

"Frika." She is known as "Frika." "Hals And Hals." "Hansel And Frika." "The Best Of Dutch Vaude—"

FRANZ

Ja, ja— Frika: I still need to cast another female. Your type. You sing?

HANSEL

She has studied voice since childhood.

FRANZ

Try a cold read from the score? You probably know this piece...

FRANZ retrieves a bound copy of the musical score, flips pages finds:

FRANZ (cont'd)

"Vilia." Famous. I'll hear you right now, if you wish. If not...

FRANZ crosses to the microphone.

FRIKA

Hansel...?

HANSEL

You know this one...

FRANZ

(Shouts into the microphone)
Give me playback number thirteen, please! And WHERE IS FRÄULEIN SONNTAG?!
(To FRIKA)
You know this one?
(FRIKA nods)
Good. Do your best.

HANSEL
(Under his breath, to FRIKA)
Diaphragm... Support it...

*A beautiful **RECORDED PIANO INTRO** (See
PRODUCTION NOTES at end of play*) to "**VILIA**" from
"**THE MERRY WIDOW**" begins. FRIKA, reading from
the score, takes a deep breath and begins to sing the song:*

FRIKA
VILIA, O, VILIA! THE WITCH OF THE WOOD.
WOULD I NOT DIE FOR YOU, DEAR, IF I—

SHE stops. SHE is awful. Cannot sing at all. SHE knows it.

*The RECORDED MUSIC playback slows to a growl,
stops. There is an awkward silence. FRIKA bows her head
in shame...*

FRANZ
Fräulein Hals, I understand this was a cold sight read; but, even so...

HANSEL
Herr Luft, do I understand correctly that, in the talking cinema, one
can synchronize an offscreen voice with the onscreen performer?

FRANZ
Young man, if you seriously believe Universum Studios would
allow me to hire two actresses for one role, you must come from
a very beautiful place.

FRIKA
It is. Holland. It is a beautiful place...

FRANZ
So I hear... Listen, I have sixteen other actresses waiting for me

to hear them today; sixteen, singing, actresses... So... Fräulein Hals, thank you, but we will not need your services. I do hate to break up your act. But...

FRIKA

Of course. I'm sorry. Take me home, please, Hansel.

FRANZ

I am not through with you, Herr Hals.

HANSEL

"Hansel." Please. Call me Hansel.

FRIKA

Hansel, please.

FRANZ

Of course, if you'd rather not continue...

HANSEL

No, no, I—

SILKE SONNTAG enters the space. SHE is in the last stages of putting on a ball gown similar to the one FRIKA is wearing. SHE's shouting at FRANZ:

SILKE

Dammit, Franz, I just took these rags off! Now you've got me all balled up!

FRANZ

Silke, I want you to meet Hansel Hals.

SILKE

Count Danilo!

FRANZ

Herr Hals: Silke Sonntag.

HANSEL

Enchanted!

SILKE and HANSEL greet each other: "air" kisses on each cheek.

SILKE

I saw you perform in Hannover, two years ago, Herr Hals. Christmastime. "Merry Widow," of course. Count Danilo! You were wonderful! I remember it to this day!

HANSEL

I have seen all of your films! Honestly! Every one! More than once! Silents and talkies! I love you! Your films, I mean! I love your films. Please, call me Hansel.

FRIKA

Hansel, *please*.

HANSEL

Frika, one moment.

SILKE
          (Referring to FRIKA)
And...?

HANSEL

Yes. My sister, Frederika. Frika.

SILKE

"Hals And Hals!" Well, of course! Enchanted...

SHE and FRIKA greet each other: "air" kisses on each cheek.

SILKE (cont'd)

The Best Of Dutch Vaudeville!

FRANZ

I am testing Hansel for the Count Danilo role.

SILKE

Testing? Franz! It's his role! He made it famous!

FRANZ

On stage, yes. For film, I test, and I want to test you two together. Right now.

SILKE

Yes. Yes! Of course!

FRANZ

Hansel?

HANSEL

I...

HE glances toward FRIKA who meets his gaze, then shrugs her shoulders, retreats toward a chair, sits.

HANSEL (cont'd)

...Yes. Yes, I'm ready.

FRANZ

(Grabs microphone and shouts:)
Give me playback number nine! Screen test, Merry Widow ballroom dance sequence: Hals And Sonntag, Take One!
(To HANSEL and SILKE)
First positions, please. Do your best...

The LIGHTS flicker again to simulate movie action

as HANSEL and SILKE assume positions. The same
RECORDED MOVIE MUSIC *from HANSEL's and*
FRIKA's screen test begins.

FRANZ (cont'd)
Action!

*HANSEL joins SILKE in a dance, the same dance HE
danced with FRIKA moments before. As earlier, the
dance soon becomes very intimate, sensual, leading to an
inevitable kiss. At the decisive moment, THEY kiss—a
passionate, romantic, kiss. The MUSIC swells and stops.
The LIGHTS change. HANSEL and SILKE linger in their
kiss ... and linger ...*

FRANZ (cont'd)
Alright, children, that will do, that will do...

*HANSEL and SILKE break from the kiss. Suddenly
FRIKA rises from the chair and bolts from the space.
HANSEL calls after her:*

HANSEL
Frika?! ... *Frika!*

Scene 2

*FRANZ and SILKE exit. LIGHTS change. HANSEL
wanders toward the dressing table. Snippets of dialogue
are heard over the monitor as HANSEL, appearing
very, very old again, sits heavily at his dressing table.
GERHART enters, as though HE's just come offstage after
a scene. GERHART sits at his dressing table and checks a
cell phone for messages.*

HANSEL

How's the house?

GERHART

Sorry, what did you say?

HANSEL

How is the house? I was nervous to look, first time out.

GERHART

Full. Typical first night.

HANSEL

They're quiet.

GERHART

Mmm. But that's good, though, no? They're listening.

HANSEL

It's supposed to be comedy... Did you try rolling your eyes, as I instructed?

GERHART

No. No, I ... I was working on something else...

HANSEL

We should be hearing laughs. This makes me very nervous.

GERHART

It will be fine! They're listening, that's all. And—and I mean no disrespect, but—maybe they don't even realize who you were. Are. Who you are.

HANSEL

They know who I am. Here, in Germany, *everyone* knows who I am.

GERHART

Well, yes, sorry, of course they do. And they'll love you. You're great in this show!

GERHART lays down his cell phone, rises from his chair.

HANSEL

Thank you.

GERHART

I'm on...

HANSEL

Yes.

GERHART leaves the dressing room. The monitor goes silent. LIGHTS change. The voice of FRIKA is heard, singing, a cappella, a German children's folk tune, "SUSE, LIEBE SUSE."

HANSEL perks up and listens. FRIKA has improved ... somewhat...

FRIKA

SUSE, LIEBE SUSE
WAS RASCHELT IM STROH?
DAS SIND DIE LIEBEN GÄNSCHEN
DIE HABEN KEINE SCHUH

HANSEL

Frika...

LIGHTS begin to illuminate FRIKA, who stands in a stylized "singing" pose, and SILKE, listening intently, who sits on a chair.

FRIKA

(Continues the song)
DER SCHUSTER HAT'S LEDER
KEINEN LEISTEN DAZU
DRUM GEHN DIE GÄNSCHEN BARFUSS
UND HABEN KEINE SCHUH

HANSEL

Frika...?

*HANSEL crosses to the microphone and speaks; his voice
blasts from the monitor:*

LAUTSPRECHER

*Waiting In The Dressing Room For His Next Cue, Hansel Hals
Thinks Of A Slightly Later, Earlier Time Than Last Time! And
He Will Do This, From Time To Time, Until Well Into Our
Second Act! So Please Continue To Believe His Memories Of
That Ancient, Ancient Past—Such As What You Are About To
Witness—Are Reasonably Reliable!*

*LIGHTS fully up on FRIKA and SILKE. FRIKA repeats
the final line of the song:*

FRIKA

DRUM GEHN DIE GÄNSCHEN BARFUSS
UND HABEN KEINE SCHUH

SILKE

You are making good progress, Frederika.

FRIKA

I hate it. It's a stupid children's song. Hansel wants me to learn more
of them—"to know the German culture better," he says. And he
wants me to sing them for him ... but I know I will be too nervous.

SILKE rises, crosses to FRIKA and embraces her.

SILKE

You shouldn't be, Frika. You are so much improved.

FRIKA

I am not.

SILKE

You only lack confidence.

FRIKA

He was right. I shouldn't be with him on the stage. Certainly not in the talking films.

SILKE

Oh, my dear Frederika...

SILKE tenderly kisses FRIKA on both cheeks. HANSEL, crossing from the microphone, shouts:

HANSEL

I never said that, Frika!

HANSEL, transformed into a much younger man, bursts in on SILKE and FRIKA.

SILKE
(Simultaneous with FRIKA)
Hansel!
FRIKA
(Simultaneous with SILKE)
Broer! (Dutch: "Brother!")

SILKE and FRIKA break apart.

HANSEL

Frika! Why are you still here?!

SILKE

Hansel. Don't scold.

HANSEL

I don't scold! Only I am surprised.

HANSEL confronts FRIKA:

HANSEL (cont'd)

And what I said, Sister, was that you are still not *ready* for the Berlin stage. Or the films. I thought you were on your way back to your teachers.

FRIKA

Ik veranderde mijn mening, Broer. Ik— (Dutch: "I changed my mind, Brother. I—")

HANSEL

Frika! Don't speak Dutch in Berlin!

FRIKA

Ik ben droevig. (Dutch: "I am sorry.")

HANSEL

Frika!

FRIKA

I am sorry! I came to tell you: I'm finished with performing. I am finished with lessons. And I am finished with Holland! I won't go back there. Everyone will laugh.

HANSEL

Oh, Frika...

SILKE

It was a stupid idea to send her back there. We have plenty of
vocal coaches here in Berlin, myself included.

HANSEL

You are too soft with her. You coddle her.

SILKE

Well, sending a young woman to Holland without proper
German papers—unaccompanied, no less? It's folly these days.
What were you thinking?

HANSEL

(To FRIKA)
You see? What did I tell you? You need a man to be with you.

FRIKA

I don't want a man.

SILKE

You hear her, Hansel? You really don't know your sister very well.

HANSEL

Here is what I *do* know: Last week, on the Platz—I saw you.
Shopping with Frika. The way you carried on with her, in public
like that...

SILKE

You are being absurd.

FRIKA

What are you talking about?

HANSEL

They recognize you, Silke. You can't hide any more. Your
reputation. *My* reputation!

FRIKA

Hide?

HANSEL

Appearances, Silke! Don't give people any more reason to talk.

SILKE

People can say what they like. I don't care.

HANSEL

But you needn't provoke!

SILKE

I am the same as when we first met, Liebchen. You loved it when I provoked!

HANSEL

It's not the Golden Twenties in Germany anymore.

SILKE

I can manage these times perfectly well, thank you, and I'll behave as I wish.

HANSEL

Please tell me you haven't taken Frika to your clubs.

SILKE

Of course I haven't! I rarely go myself. Half of them don't even exist anymore...

FRIKA

What are you talking about?

SILKE

Good question! What are you talking about, Hansel? Explain yourself, please. I can't wait to hear...

HANSEL

Frederika... You know how, in church for example, people tend to speak with disfavor about choices some others might make? About the way some people choose to live?

FRIKA

They bear false witness. They miss Easter duty. Eat meat on Fridays.

HANSEL

No, no, Frika, I mean— Well, yes, that, also, but—

SILKE laughs.

HANSEL (cont'd)

Frika, you are a young, single woman. Silke, also, single—

FRIKA

You and Silke are a couple.

HANSEL

Yes, yes, we ... we have a relationship. But she and I are not *married* to each other. You see? So. You: a single woman. Silke: also, a single woman. People see two single women... In public... You see...? Holding hands...? Sometimes ... sometimes kissing...?

FRIKA

I love Silke.

SILKE

She loves me, Hansel.

HANSEL

Frika, you... Yes, of course you, you love her. Silke is a good friend to you. But people assume there is more than friendship when they see—

FRIKA

Silke thinks I'm smart.

SILKE

You are smart.

HANSEL

Yes, of course—

FRIKA

She says I have talents.

HANSEL

You do. Yes. I'm only saying—

FRIKA

She loves to hear me sing.

HANSEL

Yes, you have a magnificent ... a decent—

FRIKA

Silke says that I can do many things, if I try.

HANSEL

No doubt, Frika. No doubt you will.

FRIKA

Then why are you so angry?

HANSEL

I'm not angry, Frika!

FRIKA

Because I have affection for Silke?

HANSEL

No, no. Affection? No. It's... Frika... I must ask you this: Are you
and Silke ... do you and Silke—?

SILKE

Stop! Now! No! NO! Don't say another word, you bastard! Don't
listen to him, Frika!

HANSEL

Frika is my sister. I have every right—

SILKE

She's your sister, not your prisoner! You have no right to
interrogate her like this!

HANSEL

I am only trying to protect her! And you as well!

SILKE

Hansel, sometimes your ignorance astonishes me.

FRIKA

(SHE is in tears)
Why are you so angry with me, brother? I am a good Dutch
Catholic girl!

HANSEL

I'm not angry!

SILKE

Hansel— Go to hell, just go to hell. And to hell with our
relationship! My reputation isn't worth one of Frika's tears. I
have friends, you know, who are just friends. Frika, won't you
please come with me? We'll go shopping again. On the Platz.
We'll walk arm in arm and greet my fans, and I will introduce
you as my great friend. Which you are, and which I hope you

always will be. We'll find real French champagne and we'll drink it and laugh while your brother stays home alone. Worrying about appearances.

SILKE and FRIKA are about to leave when SILKE turns back to HANSEL:

SILKE (cont'd)
And you can go fuck yourself, *Liebchen*. This bank is closed.

*SILKE leaves. **MUSIC** begins. HANSEL crosses to the microphone, speaks; his voice booms from the monitor:*

LAUTSPRECHER
To Dispel The Unpleasant Memory Of His Lover's Justifiable Disdain, Hansel Hals Relives A Precious Moment From His Glorious Past!

*HANSEL whirls directly to the audience. **MUSIC** begins, and HANSEL sings the same verses of "**MAXIM'S**" that HE sang in Scene One, but this time aggressively, with all the energy and vigor of a complete performer in his prime. Top hat, cane, choreography, and movie/showbiz lighting all aid the effect:*

HANSEL
I'M OFF TO CHEZ MAXIM'S
WHERE FUN AND FROLIC BEAMS!

WITH ALL THE GIRLS I CHATTER,
I LAUGH AND KISS AND FLATTER!

LOLO, DODO, JOU-JOU,
CLO-CLO, MARGOT, FROU-FROU,

FOR SURNAMES DO NOT MATTER
I TAKE THE FIRST TO HAND!

AND THEN THE CORKS GO POP!
WE DANCE AND NEVER STOP!

THE LADIES SMILE SO SWEETLY
I CATCH AND KISS THEM NEATLY!

LOLO, DODO, JOU-JOU,
CLO-CLO, MARGOT, FROU-FROU

TILL I FORGET COMPLETELY
MY DEAR OLD FATHERLAND!

> *MUSIC ends. HANSEL is out of breath from his exertion... Back at the microphone, HE sheds the showbiz props as HE speaks into the microphone:*

LAUTSPRECHER
And Hansel Hals Wants You To Know—That's How He Did It! ... You See? ... He Gave EVERYTHING For His Audiences! Held NOTHING Back! He Bled Himself Dry For His Admirers. Poor Citizens, Who Suffered ... So Terribly ... In Those Days. The World Had Changed So Quickly They Could Hardly Find Their Bearings. He Gave Them Distraction. Through His Art! Art Is Everything! When Life No Longer Makes Sense, Art Is The Only Truth! Art Will Make You Free! Kunst! KUNST MACHT FREI!

Scene 3

> *LIGHTS change, FRIKA dashes onstage. HANSEL is riveted as FRIKA addresses him:*

FRIKA
Brother, Brother, I have learned a new German song! And I am so excited! Ever since I decided to give up performing, I have lost my nervous condition! Listen...

*SHE sings a cappella "**THE WATCH ON THE RHINE.**"*
Her voice is strong, even if her pitch is a little wobbly:

FRIKA (cont'd)
THE CRY RESOUNDS LIKE THUNDER'S PEAL,
LIKE CRASHING WAVES AND CLANG OF STEEL:
THE RHINE, THE RHINE, OUR GERMAN RHINE,
WHO WILL DEFEND OUR STREAM DIVINE?
      (Suddenly moved to tears by the sentiment of the song,
      SHE sings bravely to the end:)
DEAR FATHERLAND, NO FEAR BE THINE,
LIEB' VATERLAND, MAGST RUHIG SEIN,
FIRM AND TRUE STANDS THE WATCH,
THE WATCH ON THE RHINE!
FEST STEHT UND TREU DIE WACHT,
DIE WACHT AM RHEIN!

FRIKA wipes tears from her face and smiles at the
*audience. Prerecorded **MUSIC**, resembling old-fashioned*
***RUSSIAN DANCE MUSIC**, begins. HANSEL speaks into*
the microphone:

LAUTSPRECHER
Hansel Hals Is Back Onstage Playing His Next Scene As The
Ancient Footman, FIRS, In "The Cherry Orchard." And For
Budgetary Reasons (But Also For Nuanced Artistic Effect!)
The Actress Playing FRIKA In THIS Play Will Play The Maid,
DUNYASHA, In The Play-Within-The-Play! ... Got It...?

FRIKA pulls herself together and begins to powder her
face; SHE is now playing the character DUNYASHA, the
servant girl, in a scene from Chekhov's THE CHERRY
ORCHARD (the play whose dialogue we have heard
snippets of from the monitor.) HANSEL, old again,
dressed as the footman, FIRS, the ancient family servant
in Chekhov's play, enters the "parlor." FRIKA and
HANSEL play the scene...

DUNYASHA/FRIKA

The mistress tells me to dance—there are a lot of gentlemen but few ladies—and my head goes round when I dance, and my heart beats so! The post office clerk told me something just now, Firs, that made me catch my breath.

*The **RUSSIAN DANCE MUSIC** grows faint...*

FIRS/HANSEL

What did he say to you

DUNYASHA/FRIKA

He says, "Dunyasha, you're like a little flower.'

HANSEL, as FIRS, turns out to the audience and rolls his head and his eyes in a hugely exaggerated gesture of disbelief that the serving girl should receive such a compliment. There is a burst of "audience" laughter from the monitor, which seems to please HANSEL.

DUNYASHA/FRIKA (cont'd)

"Like a little flower," Firs. I love words of tenderness.

FIRS/HANSEL

You'll lose your head. Is the coffee ready?

DUNYASHA/FRIKA

Like a little flower...

FIRS/HANSEL

You! Where's the cream?

DUNYASHA/FRIKA

Oh! Dear me!

FRIKA, as DUNYASHA, flees. HANSEL, as FIRS, shouts
after DUNYASHA:

FIRS/HANSEL

You bungler!
(HE begins to tidy up the "parlor")
The mistress... Back from Paris... The master went to Paris once ... in
a carriage! In the old days they dried the cherries from the orchard.
And then we'd send the cherries off in carts to Moscow and Kharkov.
And money! And the dried cherries were soft, juicy, and sweet...
They knew the way. But now they've forgotten. Nobody remembers...
(HE laughs)
And the mistress is home again! I've lived to see her! I don't care
if I die now... I don't care if I die...

*HE weeps with joy; the **RUSSIAN DANCE MUSIC** swells*
*then ends, then there is a sudden roaring **SOUND**. Flames*
erupt upstage, a huge bonfire casts HANSEL's form into
silhouette. HE turns toward the fire and is joined onstage
by SILKE and FRANZ. FRIKA, carrying many books,
enters, approaches the fire. SHE speaks with revolutionary
passion as HANSEL, SILKE and FRANZ watch:

FRIKA

Fellow students! Classmates! Tonight we say this with one voice:
The time has come when we must lead the fight against the
un-German spirit! We must consign everything un-German to
the fire! Therefore, against decadence and moral decay, we hand
over to the fire the writings of Thomas Mann!

There is a ROAR of approval from the monitor as FRIKA
throws books into the fire.

FRIKA (cont'd)

Against class conflict and materialism, we hand over the
writings of Karl Marx to the fire!

There is a ROAR of approval from the monitor as FRIKA throws books into the fire.

FRIKA (cont'd)
Against the overestimation of the instinctual life, we hand over the writings of Sigmund Freud to the fire!

There is a ROAR of approval from the monitor as FRIKA throws more books into the fire.

FRIKA (cont'd)
Against the tide of cultural pollution, we hand over the writings of Jack London, Upton Sinclair, Margaret Sanger, H. G. Wells, Marcel Proust and Helen Keller to the fire!

There is a ROAR of approval from the monitor as FRIKA throws more books into the fire.

FRIKA (cont'd)
Oh, and D. H. Lawrence, too!

There is a ROAR of approval from the monitor as FRIKA throws one more book into the fire.

FRIKA (cont'd)
And against Jewish science, we hand over the writings of Albert Einstein to the fire!

There is a ROAR of approval from the monitor as FRIKA throws more books into the fire.

FRIKA (cont'd)
Now the soul of the German people can again express itself! These flames illuminate the end of an old era and light up the new—when Germany will be great again! Let me hear your voices!

*There is a huge ROAR of approval from the monitor as
FRIKA throws book after book into the fire, which roars
and flares up into white, blinding, nuclear heat... When
the heat cools, FRIKA is gone.*

Scene 4

FRANZ

Twenty thousand books.

SILKE

My god.

FRANZ

Your sister is quite a powerful speaker, Hansel.

HANSEL

She ... surprises me. Often.

FRANZ

Great dramatic instincts. There could be a place for her here at
Universum.

HANSEL

She told me she believes I am wasting my talent, working for
Universum; that she despises Universum Studios for insulting
the taste and intelligence of the German people; and she hopes
the French will, as she says: "—blow Universum Studios clean
off the face of Germany and straight into Hell."

FRANZ

Aha... I see... Well... In any case, Studio business happens to be
the reason I arranged this meeting. I must ask you two to make
an important decision.

SILKE

We've decided.

HANSEL

Yes. It's clear.

FRANZ

You— It is?

SILKE

Yes. We will be married. In two weeks. It's the best decision.

FRANZ

A-ha.

HANSEL

We've come to terms. We'll have a small, civil ceremony.
The Studio could cover it as a newsreel, then a series of
newsreels over the next few months. Repeat the wedding
images. Repeat images of us at home, in the mountains, at
the cabarets, at breakfast, dinner... Repeat, repeat, repeat,
repeat...

FRANZ

I see.

SILKE

We will be a happily married, normal, couple.

FRANZ

A "Lavender" marriage...

HANSEL

A marriage.

FRANZ

Well, I am happy for you! And, I suppose, for the Studio...
Seriously: Congratulations!

SILKE

And you will be our honored guest.

HANSEL

Yes.

FRANZ

Ah, well, you see, the decision of which I was speaking—it
concerns your professional lives rather than your intimate lives...

SILKE

Oh?

FRANZ

And I am afraid I must decline your invitation. I will not be in
Berlin in two weeks' time. Nor anywhere else in Germany, for
that matter. I hope.

SILKE

Your picture! You begin next week!

FRANZ

The picture will be made, Universum assures me. But without
me as director.

HANSEL

What?!

FRANZ

And without Dafna and Barry in the lead roles...

There is a pause.

...Because...

FRANZ

Of course.

SILKE

But why without you? You are not a Jew.

FRANZ

No. No. I resigned. Solidarity, you see?

SILKE

Solidarity...

FRANZ

So. Two coveted roles have become available in my film. In *the* film, I should say. Formerly, my film. Two coveted roles for, say, a newly married, normal, couple, who also happen to be rising stars of the European cinema ... stars who, with this picture, could become like the "Super-novas" they talk about these days. Super stars. World class...
 (A pause as HANSEL and SILKE exchange looks...)
You ... are not ... Jews ... are you?

SILKE

 (Simultaneous with HANSEL)
Lutheran.

HANSEL

 (Simultaneous with SILKE)
Catholic ... lapsed...

FRANZ

So. The question: Are you interested? Of course you must discuss it. But let me emphasize: An opportunity like this may never come again. And timing, in this shitty business, is

everything. You understand me? And now is your time. You're
ready for this. You're perfect for this. And you could protect this
project for me. In my absence...

> *There is a silence as HANSEL and SILKE absorb FRANZ's*
> *words. Then FRANZ stands, prepares to leave.*

FRANZ (cont'd)

Of course; this is sudden—a burden for you, even. Talk it
over. But I am a bit pressed to plan my travel—very difficult
to arrange these days—and I wish to hand a neat package to
Universum. So. You see? Time is of the essence, in every way. By
day's end, perhaps, you might have an answer?

SILKE

Certainly, Franz.

HANSEL

By all means.

> *There is a pause...*

FRANZ

...We have come so far, my dear friends, and I will always be proud
of what we've made together. And of you. You've brought lightness—
joy, even—into this god-forsaken, miserable, tragic Realm.

SILKE

Franz...

FRANZ

Yes. You know how to contact me.

> *FRANZ exits. HANSEL and SILKE, in silence, look at*
> *each other for a moment, then embrace, giving comfort to*
> *each other.*

                                SILKE

I'm afraid, Hansel.

                                HANSEL

Don't be … don't be…

                                SILKE

What will happen?

                                HANSEL

To Franz? He'll work. In Hollywoodland.

                                SILKE

California.

                                HANSEL

They all will. Don't worry about them. They're famous. They'll
work as before. Only in a better climate. You're shaking! Are
you cold?

                                SILKE

No, I ... I just feel ... Everyone's leaving, Hansel.

                                HANSEL

Not everyone…

                                SILKE

The good ones. The smart ones. The fun ones…

                                HANSEL

We're fun…

                                SILKE

Who will direct the picture? He didn't say.

HANSEL

I don't know.

SILKE

No one as good as Franz.

HANSEL

There's plenty as good as Franz! *I* could direct!

SILKE pulls away from HANSEL.

SILKE

I can't imagine my life without him. I love him. He gave me a career.

HANSEL

And look what he's offering you now. Look what he's offering *us*.

SILKE

Dafna's and Barry's roles.

HANSEL

Don't—! No, don't think that way. They're just roles. Someone is going to take them, so why not us? Franz said it: An opportunity like this...

SILKE

We could join him. Solidarity...

HANSEL

(After a pause)
...How's your English?

SILKE

My English?

HANSEL

Actors in Hollywoodland speak English. How is your English?

SILKE

I have no English.

HANSEL

Ja. Nor I.

SILKE

We can learn.

HANSEL

And what do we do *now*, while we learn? We have no money saved. And English... It's not so easy...

SILKE is silent.

HANSEL (cont'd)

We talked about this, we *planned* for this. Married, legitimate, we could have major work, constant work, with no inquisitions.

SILKE

You'll take the role, won't you? You made up your mind as soon as Franz made the offer.

HANSEL

I... No! I—

SILKE

When have you ever refused work?

HANSEL

What?! Many times! The propaganda films? I refused them all!

SILKE

Other than those...?

HANSEL is speechless.

SILKE (cont'd)
Ja. You'll take Barry's role.

HANSEL
It's not Barry's—! ... Oh. I see... If I take the role, I'm a
collaborator. A bootlicker. Unlike, of course, Franz. Heroic
Franz.

SILKE
Don't put words in my mouth!

HANSEL
Franz is known throughout the world! He can afford his
Solidarity! Good for him! No, really, good for him. But I have
to make a living in this shitty business, too. It's all I know. So
I simply take a job that's offered to me; why not? A job not
available to Barry for reasons I have no control over! Same with
Dafna. She can't take the job, and that's no fault of yours. So
why shouldn't you have it?

SILKE
Because then the Nuremburg Laws will have worked in my
favor even though I loathe them! I'd be a willing accomplice.
And, yes—so would you!

HANSEL
May I remind you, *Liebchen*: Two weeks from now we will
sign a contract—we will willingly sign a legal contract under
the same legal system with the Nuremburg Laws... So won't
our "Lavender" marriage make us complicit in that system
anyway? Won't we profit from it, professionally, I mean...? You,
in particular...?

A pause; SILKE has no response...

HANSEL (cont'd)
I will take the role. But I will not take a political stand. As far

as the Realm is concerned, I have no opinion regarding the Nuremburg Laws. I am neutral. You are as well. And we will remain in Berlin and be married, as planned. Because it's the right thing to do. We'll use the system against itself. Our secret act of resistance. Oh, Silke, you can't let these bigots poison your future. You'd regret it forever. You know you would...

SILKE

(After a slight pause)
...I must admit—Berlin...

HANSEL

Berlin!

SILKE

They haven't completely killed this city, yet—even though they hate it. There is sanctuary here.

HANSEL

I love Berlin. My adopted home. And Berlin loves this Dutchman, too! I feel it! I love these people and they love me. And they love you! You feel it, too, don't you? I know you do! Don't you?

SILKE

Yes.

HANSEL

Don't you?!

SILKE

Yes. *Yes!*

HANSEL

And I love you!

HANSEL impulsively kisses SILKE. After a moment, SILKE breaks away, composes herself.

HANSEL (cont'd)
It will be good, Silke. We'll work, mind our own business.
Things will work out in our favor.

SILKE
Yes. But, also, maybe we study English?

HANSEL
Of course we will. So, yes! I'll telephone Franz—

SILKE
No, go in person. He has no telephone. He had it removed,
remember?

HANSEL
Ridiculous. They can't listen. How could they possibly listen?

SILKE
Go. In person. Tell him we'll do the film.

HANSEL
For the people.

SILKE
For the people.

*MUSIC begins. SILKE and HANSEL, in the exuberant
prime of their performing lives together, sing "**THE
CAVALIER**," an upbeat choreographed number from
"**THE MERRY WIDOW**" with full, garish, theatrical
lighting and spectacle:*

SILKE (cont'd)
HALLO, MAIDEN! SEE HIM RIDE,
SEE THE HORSEMAN PRANCING!

HAS HE COME TO CHOOSE A BRIDE
 FROM THE MAIDENS DANCING?

LOOK UP, MAIDEN, MARK HIM WELL!
 LEAVE THE DANCERS LONELY.

HE MAY LIKE YOU, WHO CAN TELL?
 IF HE SEES YOU ONLY!

HANSEL
SO SHE GLANCES, SHY AND SLY
 AND SHE MEETS THE HORSEMAN'S EYE!

SILKE
NOT A WORD SHE SAYS, BUT STILL,
 HE CAN TAKE HER IF HE WILL!

SILLY, SILLY CAVALIER!
 HE CAN NEITHER SEE NOR HEAR;

SILLY, SILLY HORSEMAN!
 RIDE UPON YOUR COURSE, MAN!

SILLY, SILLY CAVALIER!

HE THAT WILL NOT WHEN HE MAY
 WHEN HE WILLS IT SHALL HAVE NAY!

SILLY, SILLY HORSEMAN!
 RIDE UPON YOUR COURSE, MAN!

SILLY, SILLY CAVALIER

HALLO! HERE HE COMES AGAIN!
 SEE HIS CHARGER WHEELING!
NOW HE SEEMS A LOVELORN SWAIN,
 BEGGING AND APPEALING!

BUT THE MAIDEN, CALM AND COOL

SINGS AND DOESN'T CARE NOW!

"CAVALIER, IF YOU'RE A FOOL
I AM NOT – SO THERE, NOW!"

                    HANSEL
SO THE HORSEMAN LAUGHS, "ALL RIGHT!
IF YOU WON'T, WHY THEN, GOOD NIGHT!

PRETTY MAIDEN, NOW GOODBYE—
TAKE ANOTHER, SO WILL I!"

                    SILKE
SILLY, SILLY CAVALIER!
 YOU CAN NEITHER SEE NOR HEAR!

          SILKE (simultaneous w/HANSEL)
SILLY, SILLY HORSEMAN
          HANSEL (simultaneous w/SILKE)
CLEVER, CLEVER HORSEMAN

          SILKE (simultaneous w/HANSEL)
RIDE UPON YOUR COURSE, MAN!
          HANSEL (simultaneous w/ SILKE)
THAT'S THE PROPER COURSE, MAN!

          SILKE (simultaneous w/HANSEL)
SILLY, SILLY CAVALIER!
          HANSEL (simultaneous w/SILKE)
CLEVER, CLEVER CAVALIER!

          SILKE (simultaneous w/HANSEL)
HE THAT WILL NOT WHEN HE MAY.
          HANSEL (simultaneous w/SILKE)
YOU MAY TAKE IT AS YOU MAY.

          SILKE (simultaneous w/HANSEL)
WHEN HE WILLS IT SHALL HAVE NAY!

>   HANSEL (simultaneous w/SILKE)
> I SHALL LOVE AND RIDE AWAY!

>   SILKE (simultaneous w/HANSEL)
> SILLY, SILLY HORSEMAN
>   HANSEL (simultaneous w/SILKE)
> CLEVER, CLEVER HORSEMAN

>   SILKE (simultaneous w/HANSEL)
> RIDE UPON YOUR COURSE, MAN!
>   HANSEL (simultaneous w/SILKE)
> THAT'S THE PROPER COURSE, MAN!

>   SILKE (simultaneous w/HANSEL)
> SILLY, SILLY CAVALIER!
>   HANSEL (simultaneous w/SILKE)
> CLEVER, CLEVER CAVALIER!

HANSEL salutes SILKE, smiles, and exits. SILKE starts out after him.

>   SILKE
> SILLY, SILLY HORSEMAN!
> RIDE UPON YOUR COURSE, MAN!

> SILLY, SILLY CAVALIER!

*SHE chases after him, exits. **MUSIC** ends.*

Scene 5

GERHART, now taking the role of a BUREAUCRAT OF THE REALM and wearing a militaristic outfit, enters. HE is dragging HANSEL, who still appears to be a fairly young man, by the arm across the stage.

BUREAUCRAT OF THE REALM
Herr Hals, your sister is waiting now thirty minutes and I must
close the office!

HANSEL
Yes, forgive me, please. Filming ran late.

BUREAUCRAT OF THE REALM
We can do the work if we hurry.

*THEY arrive at a desk where LIGHTS reveal FRIKA,
who has been waiting. FRIKA is dressed in slacks and
a tailored olive-drab shirt with somewhat uniform-like
qualities. SHE rises to greet HANSEL.*

FRIKA
Hansel! You're late!

HANSEL
Forgive me. Filming—

FRIKA
You know how important this is to me!

BUREAUCRAT OF THE REALM
We have no problem, Fräulein Hals. We can accomplish this.
I am a great admirer of your brother—his beautiful wife Silke
Sonntag as well—and I am only too pleased to aid in this
process for you. Please, sit, sit.

FRIKA and HANSEL sit.

BUREAUCRAT OF THE REALM (cont'd)
Let me first, though, reaffirm what I have said in the past, so
that your brother may witness. Fräulein Hals, despite your
being an Ausländer, you—as well as your Flemish and your

Scandinavian Ausländer brothers and sisters—share Aryan blood with many of us native Germans. And I am pleased to inform you that you have been selected to receive one of the highest honors this Realm can bestow upon a female. Of course there are no medals that come with this honor. No ceremony. And much will be asked of you. Years of sacrifice will be required from you. It will be an emotionally and physically demanding service that you will be asked to provide. But there will be no others in the Realm, ever, who will have as profound an effect upon the future of our Realm, our Continent, our World, as you—you and your sisters in The Program. I am awed in your presence, may I say? And I applaud you.

The BUREAUCRAT OF THE REALM applauds FRIKA. HANSEL, slightly embarrassed, joins in.

FRIKA

Thank you, but, no, it is I who am awed.

BUREAUCRAT OF THE REALM

Yes. It is awesome. No?

FRIKA

Awesome. Yes.

HANSEL

Yes. Awesome...

BUREAUCRAT OF THE REALM

So. Herr Hals. Your sister. She is unmarried with no children, which makes her most ideal for The Program. She is free of entanglements and, shall we say, "conflicts of interest."

HANSEL

I see.

FRIKA

I am eager—

BUREAUCRAT OF THE REALM

You *are* eager. And this is why I have urged The Program
to certify you for the maximum, Fräulein Hals. We are
convinced that you will be able to service the maximum
number: Three!

FRIKA

Three!

BUREAUCRAT OF THE REALM

Three! Congratulations again. Now, as we have discussed, I
insist there must be a witness who attests that you enter into
this covenant of your own will, free of coercion. You have
chosen your brother to sign as that witness?

FRIKA

Yes.

*The BUREAUCRAT OF THE REALM holds a paper aloft
with a flourish.*

BUREAUCRAT OF THE REALM

I am excited! Are we ready then?

HANSEL

Yes.

FRIKA

Yes.

*The BUREAUCRAT OF THE REALM places the official
paper before HANSEL and hands HANSEL a pen.*

BUREAUCRAT OF THE REALM
Sign here, please.

HANSEL signs the paper and slides it across the desk to the BUREAUCRAT OF THE REALM, who then produces an 8x10 glossy publicity photo of HANSEL, holds it aloft for HANSEL to see, then slides the photo toward HANSEL.

BUREAUCRAT OF THE REALM (cont'd)
And perhaps, Herr Hals, if it is not too much trouble, and I realize how these kinds of requests must become onerous to you, but, perhaps, you might, as a favor, jot a little something here...? As a surprise for my fiancée? Perhaps...?

HANSEL
Oh. Yes. Certainly. What...?

BUREAUCRAT OF THE REALM
Oh, just your famous name ... and something else in your own words, as you see fit...

HANSEL
Of course.

HANSEL poises the pen over the photograph.

BUREAUCRAT OF THE REALM
Or you might say, "For Selma."

HANSEL
Certainly.

HANSEL begins to sign his autograph.

BUREAUCRAT OF THE REALM
"For Selma." And then, perhaps, "My best wishes." And then, perhaps, "May you please find eternal happiness with your little Willie..." Then your famous name...?

HANSEL
Certainly ... Willie...

HANSEL writes the message then slides the photo back to the BUREAUCRAT OF THE REALM, who studies the autograph for a moment, beaming; it is a prized possession.

BUREAUCRAT OF THE REALM
Thank you, Herr Hals. My Selma is your greatest admirer. Other than the Chancellor, I hasten to add! He, of course, is your greatest admirer! But my Selma, she will treasure this favor from you forever, Herr Hals. Thank you, thank you.

The BUREAUCRAT OF THE REALM slips the autographed photo into a desk drawer.

BUREAUCRAT OF THE REALM (cont'd)
And now you, please, Fräulein Hals.

The BUREAUCRAT OF THE REALM slides the official paper to FRIKA. HANSEL hands the pen to FRIKA and SHE signs.

BUREAUCRAT OF THE REALM (cont'd)
Congratulations, Fräulein Hals. You are formally accepted into The Fountain Of Life!

FRIKA, overwhelmed by the magnitude of the honor, rises unsteadily from her seat. HANSEL, too, rises and embraces his sister.

HANSEL

My dear Frika—

FRIKA pulls back from HANSEL.

FRIKA

No. No! I don't answer to that name anymore.

HANSEL

Fr— Frederika—

FRIKA

Frederika is dead. You will call me Brünnhilde.

There is a slight pause...

HANSEL

...Brünn—? But, that's...that's so—

FRIKA

Brünnhilde. That, or Sister. Nothing else. I am not now who I once was. I am not now who I may yet become.

SHE grabs HANSEL in a strong bear-hug of an embrace.

FRIKA (cont'd)

Oh, Brother! You will support me?

HANSEL

Of course I will support you, Fr— Brünn— Brünn...hilde. You know that. Silke and I, both.

BUREAUCRAT OF THE REALM

I understand, Fräulein Hals, that your first has already been selected and you will be introduced very shortly, perhaps by week's end.

FRIKA

I will prepare myself.

BUREAUCRAT OF THE REALM

So... For the Realm!

HANSEL

For ... the Realm...

FRIKA

(SHE pumps a fist in the air)
FOR THE REALM!

Scene 6

*LIGHTS begin to flicker, to simulate film on a movie
screen. FRIKA and the BUREAUCRAT OF THE REALM
exit as SILKE joins HANSEL. Behind SILKE and
HANSEL, the GRIP puts into place a scenery flat painted
to resemble an idyllic mountainscape. A disembodied*
VOICE *booms from the monitor in the style of a newsreel
voice-over:*

LAUTSPRECHER

*Universum Film stars, Hansel Hals and his vo-lup-tu-ous Frau,
Silke Sonntag, enjoy their holidays together in the mountains when
they are between films! Herr Hals enjoys bird-watching, he says.
We say: We enjoy bird-watching also—especially if the bird being
watched is Germany's very own Bird Of Paradise, Silke Sonntag!
Tweet, tweet, tweet, little bird! And what's this, now? Could it be—*

*The actor who plays FRANZ, now dressed in such a
way as to resemble ADOLF HITLER wearing vaguely
militaristic lederhosen, appears.*

LAUTSPRECHER (cont'd)

—the Chancellor himself? Yes! The Chancellor never misses an
opportunity to admire the natural beauty of the Homeland!
And today, in this charming setting, the Chancellor presents
the couple with a personally autographed copy of his best-
selling book, "My Difficulties!" And we are sure everyone in
the audience has themselves read, studied, and enjoyed, from
cover to cover, all seven hundred and sixty-nine pages of their
OWN copy of "My Difficulties." Yes? Of course you have! And
of course we all know the Chancellor Of The Realm is always
first to recognize the greatest artistic talents under Germanic
skies, so on this glorious Bavarian afternoon, the Chancellor is
proud to welcome Hansel Hals to the list of artists singled out
for recognition by the Third Realm. Yes, the Chancellor's favorite
Ausländer will become the only non-German on the God-
Endowed-Artists list, which includes recent inductees, Richard
Strauss and Karl Orff. The coveted honor of GOD-ENDOWED-
ARTIST will be officially conferred upon Herr Hals in an
upcoming State ceremony!

FRANZ/ADOLF HITLER exits.

LAUTSPRECHER (cont'd)

Wait! Our lovely little bird seems disappointed! Could she be
envious that she is not recognized as GOD-ENDOWED herself?!
Don't worry, little bird! Every man in the Realm agrees: Silke
Sonntag is God-Endowed! In all the most important places!
Tweet, tweet, tweet!

> *The flickering LIGHTS cease. The newsreel has ended.*
> *SILKE and HANSEL remain on the stage before the*
> *scenery flat, HANSEL still holding the copy of "My*
> *Difficulties."*

SILKE

You like him, don't you?

HANSEL

He's been good to me.

SILKE

But you *like* him.

HANSEL

I don't dislike him.

SILKE
(Mimicing the newsreel)
"Tweet, tweet, tweet..." If I were a bird I'd shit all over his fascist head...

HANSEL

Oh, Silke!

SILKE

"God-Endowed"? My god, Hansel—you don't really believe that, do you? "God-Endowed"?

HANSEL

It's a turn of phrase.

SILKE

You're *not*, you know ... in any sense of the phrase.

HANSEL

Don't be mean, *Liebchen*.

SILKE
Disgusting... The way you shook his hand ... received his embraces...

HANSEL
Can we help who admires our work?

SILKE

My admirers aren't murderous sadists out to rule the earth.

HANSEL

Oh, please! You may as well say they all eat little Polish babies. And secondly—

SILKE

Read the book, Hansel!

HANSEL

—and secondly, your admirers are the same as mine. National Socialists, Social Democrats, Communists, Racialists, Christian Socialists—they all love us, Silke.

SILKE

He kisses your cheeks, you beam with joy, and I gag down my vomit.

HANSEL

They love us and we have no control over that. Those thousands and thousands of sausage-eating, German brutes—ogling your glamor photos—fantasizing about all the things they could do with you in the dark... Did you choose them?—those ignorant worshippers without imagination enough to think a woman could reject them in favor of another woman? Without them, Silke, without their patronage, we are nothing. So the Chancellor patronizes me; what can I do? Nothing.

SILKE

You will go on the List?

HANSEL

I will...

There is a pause.

SILKE

...I can't understand that, Hansel. It profoundly disturbs me.

HANSEL

I have no choice! How can I *not* go on the List, now that the Realm has singled me out? How? Impossible!

SILKE

Not impossible if you publicly refuse. Go to the newspapers. Tell them you'll have no part of any ... pat on the head from a gang of thugs. You'll be off that List in an instant.

HANSEL

That would be suicide.

SILKE

Appearances, Hansel? They don't concern you anymore? You'll become their political tool, like it or not.

HANSEL

No. I'm Switzerland; I'm neutral. They know that. I entertain. That's all! I do my work and I mind my own business. And look at the company I'll join: the greatest German artists of our age. Me. A Dutchman. And you—it will reflect on you, too. Think of the publicity...

SILKE

I am thinking of it, Hansel, and I hate it. I'd rather have my old life back. My Cabaret life...

HANSEL

When they accused you of prostitution because you were single and childless? When you hid all your "Girlfriend" magazines under the carpets? Your discreet lessons with your "vocal coach?"

SILKE

She *was* my vocal coach.

HANSEL

We've never held each other to monogamy. That was never part of the arrangement.

SILKE

That's not what I mean! The exposure... And this ... *arrangement*, this ... marriage... It's exhausting. I always feel a fraud. I don't even act well anymore...

There is a pause...

HANSEL

...I'm sorry. I thought you appreciated the favor.

SILKE

What favor?

HANSEL

Marrying you? Shutting down a whole city of gossip-mongers? Sparing your career...?

SILKE

...Oh, Hansel...

HANSEL

What?

SILKE

Oh, Hansel...

HANSEL

What?

                              SILKE

I thought you loved me...

                              HANSEL

Of course I do! But, we knew what we were doing. We had no
illusions... Did we...?

                              SILKE

No. No illusions.

                              HANSEL

Well, then...

              There is a pause...

                              SILKE

...We never learned English.

                              HANSEL

English? Ah. No.

                              SILKE

We could still learn. In Hollywoodland.

       *Melancholic **MUSIC** begins: "**NOTHING AT ALL**"*

                              HANSEL

Hollywoodland...

                              SILKE

Slip away with me, Hansel. Please? To California? Maybe there,
in all that sunshine, I can feel free again.

                              HANSEL

Where do you suppose they first celebrated a "Lavender
Marriage?"

SILKE

Of course. I'm a fool. But I am, still, your wife... Be my husband,
for a while longer, anyway, won't you? Be my companion...?
Franz can help make arrangements. He only needs to know how
many will be traveling. One? Two...?

HANSEL is silent...

SILKE (cont'd)

You know, sometimes one acts ... by *not* acting...

HANSEL is silent...

SILKE (cont'd)

So. I am going back to Berlin. Finish your visit here alone, if you
wish, but please, let me know soon, won't you? My husband?
Let me know... And don't use the telephone...

*SILKE kisses HANSEL on each cheek and exits. HANSEL
directly addresses the audience:*

HANSEL

And I never saw her again...

*HANSEL sings "**NOTHING AT ALL**":*

HANSEL (cont'd)

TODAY WE ARE LOVERS
TOMORROW WE'RE STRANGERS.

YESTERDAY'S DREAMS
SWEET FATE REARRANGES.

SO STOP UP MY TEARS.
NO, WAIT, I HAVE NONE.

THEY'RE GONE LIKE ALL THOSE OTHERS
WHO HAVE LEFT ME ABANDONED.

ONE MAN, ALONE,
I HEED MY CALL.
I DO, BY DOING NOTHING

AT ALL

MUSIC ends.

Scene 7

HANSEL crosses quickly to the microphone, grabs it. HIS voice blasts from the loudspeaker:

LAUTSPRECHER
Hansel Hals Suffers A Terrifying Actor's Nightmare!

GERHART (as LOPAKHIN), SILKE (as LUBOV), and FRANZ (as GAEV) swoop into the "parlor" space, speaking lines as THEY enter. THEY are characters in Chekhov's "The Cherry Orchard"—the play-within-the-play. SILKE, FRANZ, GERHART and HANSEL will speak lines from the homecoming scene in Chekhov's play. HANSEL, still in the playing area, remains dressed as in the previous scene, but he acts very, very old, as the character FIRS. LUBOV/SILKE addresses GAEV/FRANZ as SHE begins the scene:

LUBOV/SILKE
Let me remember now. Red into the corner! Twice into the center!

GAEV/FRANZ moves his body about as if he is playing billiards...

GAEV/FRANZ

Right into the pocket! Once upon a time you and I both used to sleep in this room. We could smell the cherry orchard. And now I'm fifty-one; it does seem strange.

LOPAKHIN/GERHART

Yes, time does go.

GAEV/FRANZ

Who does?

LOPAKHIN/GERHART

I said that time does go.

GAEV/FRANZ

It smells of patchouli in here.

LUBOV/SILKE

Whew! It's getting on for three o'clock in the morning! I'll have some coffee now, then we all must go.

FIRS/HANSEL helps LUBOV/SILKE into a chair.

LUBOV/SILKE (cont'd)

I'm used to coffee. I drink it day and night. Thank you, Firs. Thank you, dear old man.

LUBOV/SILKE kisses FIRS/HANSEL

LUBOV/SILKE (cont'd)

I'm so glad you're still with us.

FIRS/HANSEL

The day before yesterday.

GAEV/FRANZ

He doesn't hear well.

LOPAKHIN/GERHART

I've got to go off to Karkhov by the five o'clock train. I'm awfully sorry. I should like to stay a bit, gossip a little.

FIRS/HANSEL

Where is that girl with the coffee?

Suddenly LUBOV/SILKE stands up from her chair and looks toward an upstage entrance.

LUBOV/SILKE

She is here! Oh! The happiness!

LOPAKHIN/GERHART and GAEV/FRANZ look upstage as well.

LOPAKHIN/GERHART

The excitement!

FIRS/HANSEL

...What? What?

GAEV/FRANZ

The honor!

FIRS/HANSEL

What are we—? This is not—

LUBOV/SILKE

She comes!

GAEV/FRANZ

She has brought them with her! Three! They gave her three!

LOPAKHIN/GERHART

Three!

LUBOV/SILKE

Three!

FIRS/HANSEL

We've gone off here, haven't we? We've gone way off. Who...?

FIRS/HANSEL looks off into the wings.

FIRS/HANSEL (cont'd)

Line...? Whose line...?

*LUBOV/SILKE, GAEV/FRANZ and LOPAKHIN/
GERHART all cheer wildly as FRIKA, dressed in her
uniform-like garb and holding three bundled babies in her
arms, enters from upstage.*

LUBOV/SILKE

Hooray!

GAEV/FRANZ

Hail!

LOPAKHIN/GERHART

Brava!

LUBOV/SILKE

Yes! Wilkommen!

GAEV/FRANZ

Wilkommen! Wilkommen!

LOPAKHIN/GERHART

Wilkommen!

FIRS/HANSEL turns toward the commotion, recognizes his sister holding the three babies.

FIRS/HANSEL

Frika?

FRIKA walks forward. SHE is smiling broadly. LUBOV/ SILKE, GAEV/FRANZ, and LOPAKHIN/GERHART surround her as they speak.

GAEV/FRANZ

Fräulein Hals, greetings from the committee!

LUBOV/SILKE

Greetings!

LOPAKHIN/GERHART

Hail!

FIRS/HANSEL

Frika, what are you doing?! We are playing a scene!

LUBOV/SILKE peers into the bundles in FRIKA's arms.

LUBOV/SILKE

Oh, look! They are beautiful! Golden!

GAEV/FRANZ and LOPAKHIN/GERHART also peer into the bundles.

LOPAKHIN/GERHART

Yes! Golden children!

GAEV/FRANZ

Golden! Yes! Golden Children!

FIRS/HANSEL

Children? CHILDREN? There are no children in this play!

LUBOV/SILKE

Fräulein Hals, we are so proud of you! So terribly proud.

FIRS/HANSEL

These are not the lines!

LOPAKHIN/GERHART

So proud. The congregation is proud of you.

GAEV/FRANZ

The entire congregation!

In an attempt to get the other cast members back on track, HANSEL speaks loudly his lines as FIRS from the scene. The OTHERS ignore him:

FIRS/HANSEL

When the Emancipation came, I was already first valet!

LUBOV/SILKE

And the congregation has asked us to form this little committee to express to you their respect.

LOPAKHIN/GERHART

Their admiration.

FIRS/HANSEL

Already first valet!

GAEV/FRANZ

Their abundant favor.

FIRS/HANSEL

I remember, everybody was happy, but they didn't know why!

GAEV/FRANZ
(To FIRS/HANSEL)
Be quiet, Firs.

HANSEL responds instantly to this cue, which he recognizes as an actual line from the scene:

FIRS/HANSEL

Ah! Aha!

FIRS/HANSEL begins diligently brushing at GAEV/ FRANZ's trousers as HE shouts his proper lines.

FIRS/HANSEL (cont'd)
You've put on the wrong trousers again, Leonid Andreyevitch! What am I to do with you?!

LUBOV/SILKE
(Still speaking to FRIKA and ignoring HANSEL)
So, a little speech has been prepared on behalf of the congregation...

GAEV/FRANZ
(To FIRS/HANSEL)
You go away, Firs! I will undress myself!

FIRS/HANSEL

Leonid Andreyevitch!

LUBOV/SILKE

...so that you will know how your unselfish sacrifice profoundly inspires us all.

FIRS/HANSEL

Leonid Andreyevitch, don't you fear God?

LUBOV/SILKE

So...

LOPAKHIN/GERHART

So...

LUBOV/SILKE and LOPAKHIN/GERHART turn toward
GAEV/FRANZ and begin to applaud him:

LUBOV/SILKE and LOPAKHIN/GERHART

Speech! Speech! Speech!

GAEV/FRANZ

Ahem. Yes. Very well...

FIRS/HANSEL

Leonid Andreyevitch! When are you going to bed?

GAEV/FRANZ

Be quiet, Firs! Ahem...

Throughout his speech, GAEV/FRANZ, as he did at the
beginning of the scene, moves his body about as if he is
playing billiards...

GAEV/FRANZ (cont'd)

Fräulein Hals, it is with a deep sense of pride—red off the rail
and into the corner!—that I have accepted the honor to be the
spokesperson for the entire congregation—

LUBOV/SILKE

Hear, hear!

FIRS/HANSEL

My God! What is happening?

GAEV/FRANZ

The congregation recognizes that the Realm has never promised you, or your sisters in The Program, the official recognition you all so richly deserve.

HANSEL again looks into the wings for help...

FIRS/HANSEL

Is anyone...? Line...? Line...? Please... Someone...

GAEV/FRANZ

The congregation also recognizes that these orphan children, these little, Golden, orphan children, are unadoptable in their own Homeland. But your congregation bears witness to the hand of God at work, Fräulein Hals, when we see you and your sisters in The Program—bank off the side rail into the green!—opening up your lives and your warm German homes to these poor, displaced innocents.

LOPAKHIN/GERHART

Hear! Hear!

LUBOV/SILKE

Hand of God!

FIRS/HANSEL

God in heaven...

GAEV/FRANZ

Therefore, Fräulein Hals, therefore—green in the corner!—the congregation hereby—tick the orange!—hereby bestows upon you—orange off the yellow-stripe—the title of—off the rail and across!—GOD FAVORED!—And into the side pocket!

LUBOV/SILKE produces a brilliantly sparkly tiara which she places on FRIKA's head.

LUBOV/SILKE

God-Favored!

LOPAKHIN/GERHART

Hear! Hear!

LUBOV/SILKE

God-favored!

GAEV/FRANZ

God-Favored!

FRIKA

Thank you! Oh! Thank you!!

FIRS/HANSEL

God...? God-favored?

FRIKA

Be quiet, Firs!

LOPAKHIN/GERHART

Three cheers!

LUBOV/SILKE

Three cheers!

GAEV/FRANZ

Three cheers for Fräulein Hals!

LUBOV/SILKE

Three cheers for Fräulein Hals and Her Many Blessings!

ALL but HANSEL raise their arms to FRIKA in a two-armed, waving, palms-to-heaven salute.

FIRS/HANSEL

This is a nightmare!

ALL but HANSEL cheer FRIKA.

ALL

For Fräulein Hals and Her Many Blessings! HURRAH! HURRAH! HURRAH!

FIRS/HANSEL

This is insane.

FRIKA

Be quiet, Firs!

HANSEL

Frika! It is I. Your brother! Hansel! I'm just acting! I am not Firs!

FRIKA

And I am not "Frika!" I am Brünnhilde!

HANSEL

And you are not in this scene! Not in this play! You are not even an actress anymore! Why are you here?

FRIKA

Because I am favored by God.

ALL
(Except HANSEL and FRIKA)

God-favored!

LUBOV/SILKE

She glows!

GAEV/FRANZ

Like a star!

HANSEL

No. This is not happening.

FRIKA

This is happening! This is real, Brother!

> As FRIKA speaks, LUBOV/SILKE relieves FRIKA of one
> of the babies and returns to her comfortable chair where
> she cuddles the infant. GAEV/FRANZ and LOPAKHIN/
> GERHART take the remaining babies from FRIKA and
> retreat upstage where THEY gently rock and comfort the
> babies.

FRIKA (cont'd)

Are not my babies real?

HANSEL

No! Well, yes, but, *these* babies? No! They are stage props!

FRIKA

Is not this committee real?

HANSEL

Real? No! They are actors!

FRIKA

Is not this tiara real?

HANSEL

It is a stage prop, Frik— Brünn—

FRIKA

Is not the admiration of my congregation real?

HANSEL

Well, yes, that—

FRIKA

Is not the respect given me by the Realm real?

HANSEL

Yes, yes. Of course—

FRIKA

Are not the newsreels that praise me and my sisters in The Program real?

HANSEL

Yes. They are—

FRIKA

The newsreels they show before your films?

HANSEL

Yes.

FRIKA

The newsreels that show the multitudes who celebrate The Program, the good work we do, the patriotic sacrifices we sisters endure?

HANSEL

Real. All real.

FRIKA

And the roars of approval from the throats of audiences who witness me and my sisters in The Program as we adopt and save these little, innocent, orphaned Polish infants; are they not as real as can be, Brother?

HANSEL

Real. Yes. I have heard them roar.

FRIKA

I have heard them roar, too, Brother. And I love the sound. May it deafen me! That sound has mass. Weight. Like the solid Earth itself. Where I can stand. Supported by that thrilling roar! And where I stand now is my territory, Brother. Mine! I claim it. I own it. And I will defend it. From all intruders, Brother—even you. Especially you. You have your own territory, with Silke. Let me have mine. Please...?

FRIKA becomes overwhelmed with joy—near tears with emotion. SHE is radiant, glowing (literally, thanks to the lighting designer).

FRIKA (cont'd)

Oh, my Brother! Love begets Love! I love my babies—my congregation loves me! I love my Fatherland—my Fatherland loves me! I love the people! And the people—they love me! Just as they love you! Oh, it feels so right to be here. You know the ecstasy of being on stage. But I never knew, till now. At long last, I have arrived here with you! Equal with you! And I love it here, Brother. I belong here! I swear to you, I swear to all the universe, I will never be anywhere else. I would not be able to go on living.

HANSEL

I understand, Sister.

FRIKA

I know you understand. We are the same in this way.

HANSEL

Brother...Sister...the same. My blood flows in your veins and yours in mine.

FRIKA

Your eyes open and my mind sees.

HANSEL

You sip from the cup and I taste the wine. The same.

FRIKA

The very same... Heavenly bodies... Like twin stars...

FRIKA comes to HANSEL and kisses him on the mouth. The radiance that surrounds FRIKA briefly illuminates HANSEL. For a moment THEY are twin stars... Then FRIKA releases HANSEL, who stands stunned as FRIKA calls out:

FRIKA (cont'd)

My babies. I want my babies. My Golden Children. I love them so very much…

LUBOV/SILKE, GAEV/FRANZ and LOPAKHIN/ GERHART each return a baby to FRIKA. She peers into the bundles.

FRIKA (cont'd)

...so very much. My Golden Children... Wilkommen...

FRIKA continues to speak as she exits.

FRIKA (cont'd)

Wilkommen. You are home at last, my Golden Children... Golden Hair... ice-blue eyes...

FRIKA exits. ALL resume their actual lines from the scene.

GAEV/FRANZ
And...smack! Corner pocket!

LOPAKHIN/GERHART
(Sings a little snippet of a tune)
"...for money will a German make a Frenchman of a Russian..."
(Laughs)
I saw such an awfully funny thing at the theater last night!

LUBOV/SILKE
Firs...? Firs?!

*HANSEL, dazed, tries to re-focus his attention on playing
the scene in his role as ancient FIRS.*

FIRS/HANSEL
Mistress?

LUBOV/SILKE
Firs, if the cherry orchard is sold, where will you go?

FIRS/HANSEL
I'll go wherever you order me to go, Mistress.

LIGHTS begin to fade on all but HANSEL...

LUBOV/SILKE
Why do you look like that, Firs? Are you ill? I think you ought to go to bed...

FIRS/HANSEL
Yes. Yes. I'll go to bed... And who'll handle things around
here and give orders without me? I've the whole house on my
shoulders... The whole house... On my shoulders...

BLACKOUT
END OF ACT ONE

ACT 2
Scene 1

*As HOUSE LIGHTS fade, pageant-like **MUSIC** begins.
When the theater is in complete darkness, a disembodied
VOICE booms over the MUSIC from the monitor:*

LAUTSPRECHER
*Meine Damen und Herren, Ladies and Gentlemen, Guten Abend,
und Wilkommen! Welcome to... The Realm Honors!*

Tympanies thunder, thrilling chords are struck.

LAUTSPRECHER (cont'd)
*Tonight, the Realm honors the life, the career, the achievements
of one of Germany's most celebrated performers, a truly God-
Endowed Artist, hereafter to be recognized as Gottbegnadeten:
Herr Hansel Hals!*

*Applause thunders from the monitor, and suddenly
a movie screen flickers to life, lit by a filmmontage of
HANSEL HALS in scenes from maybe a dozen of his
films. HE is seen, and heard, singing, dancing, laughing,
crying, shouting, kissing. Many of the scenes are two-shots
of HANSEL and SILKE SONNTAG. From the monitor
come audience reactions: laughing at the funny scenes,
cheering at the dancing and singing, occasional booing
when SILKE appears, etcetera. When the final image, a
closeup of a beaming HANSEL HALS, appears on the
screen, the MUSIC stops and the LAUTSPRECHER
announces:*

LAUTSPRECHER (cont'd)
*And now, Ladies and Gentlemen, please acknowledge this God-
Endowed Artist, our Chancellor's favorite Dutchman...Herr
Hansel Hals!*

*Triumphal **MUSIC** begins. Huge applause pours from
the monitor as the full stage is suddenly awash with light,
revealing flowing red banners with huge Nazi swastikas
hanging from a balcony. Sitting side by side in the center
of the balcony are HANSEL and ADOLF HITLER (played
by the actor who plays FRANZ). HANSEL, smiling as
broadly as in the final film image, rises from his seat and
acknowledges the cheers of the crowd. HANSEL turns and
shakes hands with ADOLF HITLER, who rises and kisses
HANSEL on both cheeks. The monitor blares the voices of
the throng as they cheer:* "**Hail! Hail! Hail!**" *HANSEL and
ADOLF HITLER resume their seats. The MUSIC stops.*

LAUTSPRECHER (cont'd)
*Ladies and Gentlemen, now please welcome to the stage the
Realm's most celebrated film director...Leni Riefenstahl!*

*Applause from the monitor as **MUSIC** ushers in LENI
RIEFENSTAHL (played by the actor who plays SILKE
SONNTAG) who comes center stage.*

LENI RIEFENSTAHL/SILKE
Danke. Danke. Thank you. *Danke! Nein! Bitte!* Thank you!
Danke... Danke...

*Applause finally ends. LENI RIEFENSTAHL speaks
directly to the audience. HANSEL and ADOLF HITLER
react to LENI throughout her speech.*

LENI RIEFENSTAHL/SILKE (cont'd)
God-Endowed... *Gottbegnadeter...* God-Endowed... *Gott im
Himmel*, are you kidding me? This guy? God-Endowed? I've
seen him in the shower! Ha ha ha!

*HANSEL and ADOLF HITLER laugh, punch each other
in the arm, etcetera, as laughter spews from the monitor.*

LENI RIEFENSTAHL/SILKE (cont'd)
Nein, nein, nein! I'm joking! But ... a girl can dream! Eh, ladies?!
Ha ha ha! But seriously, seriously, I do have it on good authority
that Herr Hals, unlike some others I could mention, has *two*
balls! Ha ha ha!

> *HANSEL and ADOLF HITLER laugh, punch each other
> in the arm, etcetera, as laughter spews from the monitor.*

LENI RIEFENSTAHL/SILKE (cont'd)
Seriously! It takes a pair of brass ones to order two thousand
five hundred Panzer Tanks to invade France! Am I right? Huh?
Am I right?! So: Hail to the Chief!

> *HANSEL and ADOLF HITLER laugh, punch each other
> in the arm, etcetera, as laughter spews from the monitor.*

LENI RIEFENSTAHL/SILKE (cont'd)
And congratulations to Herr Hals for making the distinguished
Gottbegnadeten Liste. Congratulations, Dutchman! What is it
the Dutch say? "We may not be as smart as the Germans, but at
least when we hear a knock on the door before dawn, we know
it's only the milkman!"

> *HANSEL and ADOLF HITLER laugh, punch each other
> in the arm, etcetera, as laughter spews from the monitor.*

LENI RIEFENSTAHL/SILKE (cont'd)
Gottbegnadeter? Gesundheit! Ha, haa! *Nein, nein!* Seriously,
congratulations, Herr Hals! I have known you since I made
my first film; admired your artistry, your many, many, God-
Endowed talents. I'm a huge fan. Huge. Huge fan. You know,
ladies and gentlemen, I have tried over and over to cast Herr
Hals in films I've made for the Realm, but he's always refused
me. Actually expected to be paid! Never had that problem with
the Gypsies from the Resettlement Camps!

HANSEL and ADOLF HITLER laugh, punch each other
in the arm, etcetera, as laughter spews from the monitor.

LENI RIEFENSTAHL/SILKE (cont'd)
Y'know, there's a reason we call those Romani Gypsies in our
films "Extras": There's a ton of 'em, and they're all disposable!

HANSEL and ADOLF HITLER laugh, punch each other
in the arm, etcetera, as laughter spews from the monitor.

LENI RIEFENSTAHL/SILKE (cont'd)
I will introduce the Honoree himself in just a moment. But first,
speaking, I believe, for filmmakers and film actors across the
Homeland, let me thank the film critics of the Realm who have been
so generous with their praise of our work these past few years—my
work especially. Thank you. Thank you. As I maintained all along,
before the Nuremberg Laws purged them from the ranks of your
profession, a Jewish film critic is like a schwanz up an arsehole: He's
totally missed the mark, and he's completely full of shit!

HANSEL and ADOLF HITLER laugh, punch each other
in the arm, etcetera, as laughter spews from the monitor.

LENI RIEFENSTAHL/SILKE (cont'd)
And now, *Meine Damen und Herren,* with no further delay,
may I introduce to you the man of the hour, the latest honoree
of The Realm Honors, the most recent to join the ranks of
Germany's National Treasures, and forever hereafter to be
known as *Gottbegnadeter...* Herr... HANSEL... HAL-L-L-L-S!

*Triumphal **MUSIC** plays, cheering erupts from the*
monitor. LENI, applauding HANSEL, backs away
upstage. ADOLF HITLER rises to give a standing ovation to
HANSEL, who rises, thanks ADOLF HITLER, then makes
his way down to center stage. SOUND from the monitor
decreases as the LIGHTS change until...

Scene 2

HANSEL stands alone in a spotlight center stage. Darkness surrounds him. The monitor has gone silent...

HANSEL

Danke. Thank you. *Danke.* This is a great honor. When I came from South Holland to Berlin to make my first film, a silent film, I—

There is the SOUND of a ringing telephone.

HANSEL (cont'd)
—from, from South Holland—

The telephone rings again.

HANSEL (cont'd)
—silent ... silent film—

The telephone rings a third time.

HANSEL (cont'd)
Yes? Hallo...? Hallo...? Who is this...?

FRIKA

Hansel?

HANSEL

Brünn— Brünn-hilde?

FRIKA appears, spotlit, somewhere on the set. SHE is crying.

FRIKA

Brother...

HANSEL

Sister? What is the matter? Why are you crying?

FRIKA

(Sobs)
The children — It's — Horrible—

HANSEL

Brünnhilde, I cannot understand you. Don't cry. I am here. Has
something happened to the children... Brünnhilde...?

FRIKA

Dead!

HANSEL

My god!

FRIKA

Never call me by that name again! Brünnhilde is DEAD! Up in
flames. On the funeral pyre.

HANSEL

Yes, yes, okay ... Frika, okay. And you are at your apartment?
And where are the children, Frika? Are they with you?

FRIKA

Asleep.

HANSEL

In the apartment?

FRIKA

Golden angels. At rest. At peace.

(Tries to hold back tears)
Oh, I was so happy...

                    HANSEL
At ... "at peace?" What do you mean?

                    FRIKA
But they lied to me, Brother.

                    HANSEL
Who?

                    FRIKA
To all of us.

                    HANSEL
Frika, please! Who lied? ... Frederika!

                    FRIKA
Oh, Hansel!
          (Bursts into tears again)
They are not dead—

                    HANSEL
Not dead. Good. Yes. Okay. So why—

                    FRIKA
They said they were dead. From the invasion.

                    HANSEL
My god, Sister, I don't know what you're saying!

                    FRIKA
Poland! *Poland!* The parents!

HANSEL

Parents?

FRIKA

The Program. The Fountain Of Life. The children have parents. They were all taken away. Kidnapped!

HANSEL

No. No. The children were orphaned.

FRIKA

I have word from Silke. She knows things now. I have made a terrible sin!

HANSEL

Silke? Where is she?

FRIKA

She knows what The Program really is. The liars! London. She wants me to come. The Fountain Of Life takes the Golden Babies.

HANSEL

Golden—?

FRIKA

The Polish Aryans! With the golden hair! And the ice-blue eyes! Kidnapped. To be Germanised. I am guilty, Brother!

HANSEL

No. No, Frika.

FRIKA

Silke wants me to come to London. Will you come as well? Please, Hansel? Help me? I don't think I can manage alone. Silke knows everything. The Jews? The Homosexuals? Do you know where they go? The Bisexuals? Do you know what happens to them, Hansel?

HANSEL

Well, you mean ... the resettlement camps...?

FRIKA

The camps! Yes! And the killing! They are killing them, Hansel!

HANSEL

Calm down now, calm down!

FRIKA

It's on the BBC! Silke says!

HANSEL

The BBC. Frika, sometimes there are fake stories. You can't—

FRIKA

Churchill said it! Silke told me! On the radio! They are killing them!

There is a pause...

HANSEL

...It's just ... I've heard the stories, of course, but it's difficult to imagine. So many people? Maybe it's true, but— Oh god! Frika!

FRIKA

Hansel?

HANSEL

You telephoned me!

FRIKA

Yes—

HANSEL

We can't discuss any of these things over the telephone!

FRIKA

Why are you angry?

HANSEL

We should ring off, Frika! Now!

FRIKA

But, I need you—

HANSEL

We mustn't speak! Not on the telephone! Stay there—

FRIKA

OH—!

LIGHTS suddenly blackout on FRIKA. **MUSIC** *begins:*
"NEUTRAL MAN."

HANSEL

...Frika...? ...Frederika...? ...Sister...?

Scene 3

*LIGHTS come up on SILKE. HANSEL remains in place.
SILKE sings* **"NEUTRAL MAN:"**

SILKE

HE'S NEUTRAL MAN
HAS NO AFFILIATION
DOES ALL HE CAN
FOR HIS WEARY NATION.

HE SEES ALL SIDES
OF ALL SITUATIONS
DOES WHAT HE MUST
TO MAINTAIN GOOD RELATIONS.

AND WHEN IT COMES
 TO MAKING CHOICES
HE GIVES THE FLOOR
TO THE LOUDEST VOICES.
        (Spoken:)
Is that any way to act, I ask you...?

        (Sings:)
HE THINKS THE WORLD
COULD NEVER WORSEN
IF HE SEES GOOD
IN EV'RY PERSON.

AND WHEN THEY CHEER
 AND PAY HIM FAVOR
 THAT'S ALL HE ASKS:
THIS SIMPLE GIFT TO SAVOR.

FOR HE KNOWS HE'S JUST A TOOL,
 THE MEANS TO A DISTANT END,

WHEN ALL THE STRIFE AND ANGST
 IS FAR BEHIND.

THEN ALL THE WORLD WILL KNOW
 JUST WHAT HE DID FOR THEM

BY WORKING HARD
 AND STAYING
 UN-ALIGNED.
        (Spoken:)
Oh, he's in the shit now...

(Sings:)
HE THINKS THE RULE,
 "DO UNTO, AND BE DONE BY",
THE NOBLEST CODE
 OF LIVING TO BE COME BY.

NOW COMES THE SHOCK
 WHEN HE DISCOVERS
THAT HIS BELIEFS
 ARE NOT SHARED BY OTHERS...
        (Spoken:)
I told him: Don't trust the telephone...

MUSIC ends. SILKE exits.

Scene 4

*LIGHTS spread to reveal the BUREAUCRAT OF
THE REALM in his office, as in Scene 4 of Act 1.
HE is now dressed in full military uniform, with
the "SD" ("Sicherheitsdienst" ["Security Agency"])
patch on the shoulder. Lots of leather, medals, boots,
etcetera. HANSEL, still standing center stage, is in the
BUREAUCRAT's office.*

BUREAUCRAT OF THE REALM
Frederika. Frederika... I have always liked that name. My brother-
in-law—my wife Selma's brother? His name is Frederik. He has
a very sympathetic quality. Something soft about him. Very
nice. I don't mean to suggest feminine; quite the opposite. But,
appealing. I remember your sister, the day she signed the papers
for The Fountain Of Life. I remember thinking: "How soft! But
strong, too! Very appealing!" Frederik. Frederika. Soft. Strong...
        (Laughs)
But you know her best, don't you, Herr Hals? What do I

know! Oh, and let me say — my wife Selma still treasures that photograph you inscribed for her that day... how many years ago, now? She keeps it in a cedar chest along with memorabilia from our wedding day. Has refused offers to sell it for many, many Reichsmark!

HANSEL

That's... I am touched.

BUREAUCRAT OF THE REALM

And I do believe I may accurately report that, even after all these years of marriage, we remain happy. I with my little Selma, and she with—

HANSEL

Her little Willie. I am pleased to hear that. Congratulations.

BUREAUCRAT OF THE REALM

Danke schön.

HANSEL
(Indicates BUREAUCRAT's attire)

And you... You have ... advanced.

BUREAUCRAT OF THE REALM

Yes. The Realm has looked favorably upon my meager talents. I confess, I feel slightly guilty! Humbled, actually. So I try my very best, every day, to be worthy of the honor. And in that spirit I am led back to the reason for your presence before me here in an SD office, which is to say—and thank you for so promptly complying with my request—which is to say, your sister...

HANSEL

Yes.

BUREAUCRAT OF THE REALM
Do you know where she is?

There is a pause.

HANSEL
...You don't know?

BUREAUCRAT OF THE REALM
Do you know?

HANSEL
No! I don't monitor my sister's every—

HANSEL heaves a great sigh...

HANSEL (cont'd)
—You see, this surprises me. Isn't The Program supposed to take good care of the women, the children? Provide for their needs and comfort? Keep track of their whereabouts?

BUREAUCRAT OF THE REALM
You know, one of my minor regrets...? I never met your wife.

HANSEL
My— Silke?

BUREAUCRAT OF THE REALM
Is she happy?

HANSEL
Silke Sonntag?

BUREAUCRAT OF THE REALM
Yes. Making movies?

HANSEL

I have no idea.

BUREAUCRAT OF THE REALM

With the Jews who left before her?

HANSEL

I've heard no more than anyone—

BUREAUCRAT OF THE REALM

The so-called "Exiled Artists?"

HANSEL

So I wouldn't—

BUREAUCRAT OF THE REALM

Now, you, Herr Hals, are an Artist! God-Endowed. You should have medals like mine. All over your chest! For all to see when you walk down the street!

HANSEL

Well, thank you, but—

BUREAUCRAT OF THE REALM

But your face is enough, eh? What need have you of medals? Citizens recognize you by your handsome, Dutch, face! It's your bread and butter, that handsome, Dutch, face. You protect it, no? Get plenty of sleep? Stay out of fist-fights? Careful when you shave with a sharp, sharp razor?

HANSEL

I try to live a normal life.

BUREAUCRAT OF THE REALM

Do you know where she is?

HANSEL

Silke? I don't know. California, I presume.

BUREAUCRAT OF THE REALM

Frederika. Do you know where *she* is?

HANSEL

Why do you ask me?! We are siblings, not marriage partners!

BUREAUCRAT OF THE REALM

(Laughs)

Ha-haa! I think I see the problem! The misunderstanding. Really, I should interrogate more precisely. *Question*, I should say: *question* more precisely. So, listen to me closely, now. Pay attention, very careful attention, to my in-flec-tion. Are you ready? Now, I will ask you: Do you KNOWWWWWW ... where she IS...?

There is a pause.

BUREAUCRAT OF THE REALM (cont'd)

Because if you KNEWWWWWW ... where she WAS ... with the little CHILLL-dren...

HANSEL

Once and for all, I don't know where they are! Why would I hide such information from you?

BUREAUCRAT OF THE REALM

(Laughs)

Ha-haa! Now you surprise me, Herr Hals. You are an actor. Is it not your ... art ... to interpret words that are not necessarily your own? Discover intention behind syntax?

HANSEL

Have you taken her somewhere?

BUREAUCRAT OF THE REALM
I? No. Of course not!

HANSEL
You! The Realm! Where is she?!

BUREAUCRAT OF THE REALM
You are exhibiting a surprising bit of temper, Herr Hals. In a *Sicherheitsdienst* office, no less.

HANSEL
I... I'm sorry, I... I am telling you again, I have no idea where she is. I went to her apartment, more than a month ago now, and it was locked. No one answered. Neighbors told me the apartment was vacant and being remodeled. The landlady wouldn't even speak to me. So you must believe me: I know nothing; I have heard nothing; I have seen nothing! I have no information whatsoever to give you!

BUREAUCRAT OF THE REALM
Oh, I don't need any information from you. I know where she is...

HANSEL
What?!

BUREAUCRAT OF THE REALM
I—know—where—she—is. And the children, of course. I was simply asking if *you* knew where she is.

HANSEL
What have you done with them?

BUREAUCRAT OF THE REALM
I have done nothing! WE have done nothing. Herr Hals, the Realm loves you. The Realm honors you.

We would never do any harm to a National Treasure. Nor to the sister of a National Treasure. Nor to the three adoptive nephews of a National Treasure. What are you implying, Herr Hals? Really! On behalf of myself, the Realm, and the *Reichsführer,* I must say, we are a little bit offended!

HANSEL

Where are they?

BUREAUCRAT OF THE REALM

Oh ... in Heaven ... with the Angels, I suppose you might say.

HANSEL

No. My god, no... Are they dead?

BUREAUCRAT OF THE REALM

Dead? Dead? No!

HANSEL

Where is she?!

BUREAUCRAT OF THE REALM

California, of course!

HANSEL

Frika! Not Silke! Frika! Where is Frika?

BUREAUCRAT OF THE REALM

Please, keep your voice down, Herr Hals. You can be heard all the way to the Brandenburg Gate... I hoped to surprise you with helpful information. With good news! But you're somewhat spoiling the effect. Now I am telling you: She —Frika—also known as Frederika—briefly known as...
(Chuckles)
"Brünnhilde"—your sister—is in California. "Heaven On Earth" by some people's accounts. So: They are in ... Heaven—you see?

In Heaven with the— Do you have any Spanish, Herr Hals?

>   (Pronounces the name of the city in a flawless Spanish
>   accent:)

Los Angeles. Los ... Angeles... The Angels... *Die Engel...* Holly-
wood-land? Yes. "Holly-wood..." Hmm... Our German word is
so much more pleasing to the ear, don't you think? *Stechpalme.*
Stechpalme. Mmmmmmm, you can almost smell the leaves,
hmm...? Scratch them a bit, sniff your fingers...

>   (Demonstrating the action of scratching leaves and
>   smelling his fingers)

...Mmmmmmmmm... After her abrupt disappearance last
month, she emerged in London. Shared a small apartment for
nine days there with your beautiful wife. She—your sister—
received medical attention in London for burns she had sustained
earlier, here in Berlin. Seems she had injured herself while
attempting to extinguish a fire in her apartment. Lost most of her
hair to the flames. Three weeks ago, she and the boys evacuated
London and were assisted in their travel to California—
Hollywoodland; your wife, your sister, and the three Polish
children. *Such beautiful boys!* Learning to speak English now, one
supposes. Too bad. Difficult language. Illogical. Guttural.

HANSEL

Why did you call me here? If the SD had that intelligence, why
have you been interrogating me?

BUREAUCRAT OF THE REALM

Ja, sorry, Herr Hals, very sorry. My training. We call it *"Katz
und Maus."* I, *Katz*—you, *Maus.* I play a little with the subject,
subject weakens a little for me. Gives me some information.

HANSEL

But I have no information!

BUREAUCRAT OF THE REALM

Ja, ja. I'm afraid I'm a bit like the circus elephant, eh? I just do my act out of habit! Or like a war horse, hmm? Or—what do you have? In the theater? An old ... Buskin? Something...?

HANSEL

Trouper. An Old Trouper.

BUREAUCRAT OF THE REALM

Ah. But, in my defense, Herr Hals, truthfully, at the mention of the topic of your sister, you did exhibit the classic marks of a guilty conscience: Quick temper; little or no eye-contact; heavy sighs; paranoia... Naturally, my interrogator's instincts were aroused. And we're all guilty of... well, of something! Are we not, Herr Hals? Or, were you acting?! Of course! We are both students of human nature. You know the tell-tale signs as well as I, or any other SD officer! But, wait— No. No. Why would you deliberately affect guilt? Makes no sense So one is tempted to believe, perhaps, yes, you are guilty of something! Admitted certain heretical doubts to someone. Covered up knowledge of, oh, let us say, an attempted emigration—

HANSEL

For Christ's sake! I was summoned to an SD office! Anyone would be paranoid!

BUREAUCRAT OF THE REALM

Why so? We are SD, not *Gestapo*—
        (Laughs)
—for Christ's sake!

HANSEL

No, you're not *Gestapo*, but I know you listened on Frika's tele—

HANSEL stops speaking abruptly. There is a long pause...

BUREAUCRAT OF THE REALM
... Frika's "tele?" Frika's..."tele?" Tele...scope? Tele...graph? Tele...
type? Tele...vision...?

There is another pause.

BUREAUCRAT OF THE REALM (cont'd)
... Mmm... You inspire me, you know.

HANSEL
Do I now?

*The BUREAUCRAT OF THE REALM takes a sheet of
paper from his desk, crosses to HANSEL.*

BUREAUCRAT OF THE REALM
This is all going to shit, Herr Hals. The war, the Realm, the
Chancellor—all down the crapper. And I could not possibly
care less about your sister's goddamned tele-phone. Or
what you may or may not have said over your cock-sucking
telephone ... a transcript of which I happen to have right here...

*HE begins to read from the paper, mimicking FRIKA's
voice in falsetto and HANSEL's voice in deep baritone.*

BUREAUCRAT OF THE REALM (cont'd)
...there's Frederika saying: *"Brünnhilde is DEAD! Up in flames.
On the funeral pyre."*
(Snorts with laughter)
Oh, the picture I see! Your *dummkopf* sister re-enacting
Brünnhilde's immolation scene! Third-rate opera in her
squalid little apartment; those beautiful little Polish boys as
audience! Quite the amateur actress, your sister! Yes? And her
hair goes up in flames! Too rich! Too rich! ... And she goes on:
"Kidnapped!" And, *"Silke knows what The Program really is!"*
And, *"The children have parents!"* *"The Fountain Of Life takes the*

Golden Babies!" "To be Germanised!" "Silke wants me to come to London!" And, "Jews!" "Homosexuals!" "Bisexuals!"
(Laughs)
Ha! "Bisexuals." Either one is, or one isn't, yes...? "The killing!" "CHURCHILL!" So forth and so on, then—oh, yes, then there is ... YOU: "The resettlement camps." "Maybe it's true." Ooooh! tsk! tsk! tsk! Such words from a God-Endowed, Herr Hals! Not such a good example for your admiring fan base. And ... oh, yes, your sister: "Will you come as well? Please, Hansel? Help me? I don't think I can manage alone..." Now, Herr Hals, the Realm, as you know well, looks with disfavor upon the abetting of an unauthorized emigration. So now I am looking here for where you say to her, "No, Frederika. The Realm does not approve of unsanctioned emigration..." Hmm... Hmm... Hmm... Not here! Only, "Oh god! We can't discuss any of these things over the telephone!"

HE comes very close to HANSEL and speaks with great urgency.

BUREAUCRAT OF THE REALM (cont'd)
Months ago, maybe, before this Third Realm turned to stinking excrement in my hands, I would have been obliged to execute unpleasant measures, Herr Hals... But here, now, is how large a crap I give:

HE rips the paper into neat little pieces as HE speaks.

BUREAUCRAT OF THE REALM (cont'd)
Rumors infest the Realm now. Like crabs in a whore's pussy. "Oh, the SS are raping the Polish women! Oh, the *Schutzstaffel* wants to make little Aryan babies with them! Oh, the little blond babies are being kidnapped! Oh, they're killing Jews! Oh, they're killing the Homos! Oh, the Russians are coming, the Russians are coming!" So one insignificant cipher of a dimwit Dutch girl decides to slip our Homeland with three Polish children

and a head full of rumors? What do I care? Nothing. Nothing! Less than nothing! Let her go. Let them all go—all the tens of millions of them. I have no will to stop them anymore. Can I secure a Homeland that fears its own citizens...? But you, Herr Hals—you inspire me. You love the population. Unbelievable! We Neanderthalic Germans! You give your heart and soul to us and ask nothing more in return than our willing attendance. So simple. So pure. And we shower you with favor. You inspire me. I have a favor to ask of you—the reason I summoned you to my office in the first place ... not about your sister ... the tapped telephone. Screw that. I wished only to ask a favor of you.

HANSEL

A favor.

BUREAUCRAT OF THE REALM

Yes. I like to think I am somewhat like you, Herr Hals. I have given my life to the Realm—the Realm has rewarded me. I am where I am today because ... I love my people. My colleagues. I can hardly bear to see how they suffer. The Russians *are* coming—racing to the Reichstag. This Realm is kaput. The gallows is built. We are only waiting for the noose. It kills me to see the agony in the faces of my friends. I want to help them. And I turn to you to help me. Will you? Will you do me a favor, Herr Hals?

HANSEL

What kind of favor?

BUREAUCRAT OF THE REALM

A little show? A little performance?

HANSEL

I see.

BUREAUCRAT OF THE REALM

One performance. An hour. No more.

HANSEL

It's not so easy—

BUREAUCRAT OF THE REALM

For my suffering friends? Grant them a single hour in which
they may forget their misery?

HANSEL

You twist my arm, threaten me, blackmail me, to gain a favor?

BUREAUCRAT OF THE REALM

Twist—? Black—? How? I have simply, generously, shared
information with you, Herr Hals. That is all. Blackmail? No, no,
no! These men love you, Herr Hals! You have given them a gift
no other man in the Realm could match: Distraction from their
terrible duties in a time of war! And to witness your great talent
in person, to breathe the same air as their hero breathes, to
huddle with you beneath the ragged canvas of their weary tent,
maybe even break bread with you... Why, not even brutal death
could snuff out their happiness, they love you so...

There is a pause...

HANSEL

Well... I wouldn't necessarily refuse, but... The details would
need to be discussed. The Studio would need to grant—

BUREAUCRAT OF THE REALM

Easily taken care of. Our Homeland's Security Department
still has a few connections. All expenses would be paid. Your
travel to the location, your accommodations a stipend. Just one
performance. Please...?

HANSEL

What location?

BUREAUCRAT OF THE REALM

A little town southwest of here. In upper Bavaria. The guards there, they languish. Supplies to the Camp are irregular; their quarters are spartan. Their duties onerous.

HANSEL

What little town?

BUREAUCRAT OF THE REALM

You've heard of it, probably. Dachau...?

Scene 5

The Concentration Camp at Dachau.

MUSIC begins.

The BUREAUCRAT OF THE REALM is joined by three SS GUARDS (played by the actors who play SILKE, FRIKA and FRANZ) who cheer, stomp and whistle. HANSEL leaps to the top of what was the BUREAUCRAT's desk, turns straight out to the audience. The SS GUARDS laugh and applaud as HANSEL sings for them the complete version of "MAXIM'S" and dances energetically as he performs for the SS GUARDS:

HANSEL

Thank you. thank you, thank you! Now I will sing for you my trademark song, from Lehar's famous operetta—my very favorite, and the Führer's favorite as well—"The Merry Widow!" I hope you like it!

HE sings:

HANSEL (cont'd)

MY FATHERLAND, IT IS FOR THEE
I OUGHT TO WORK FROM ONE TO THREE;

THOUGH, AS THERE ISN'T MUCH TO DO
I ONLY COME AT HALF-PAST TWO!

BUT WORKING SO EXHAUSTS A MAN,
AND I TAKE ALL THE REST I CAN.

I NEED A SLEEP TO PUT ME RIGHT
AND THAT'S WHY I SIT UP ALL NIGHT!

I'M VERY BUSY AT MY CLUB
I'LL BET A HUNDRED ON THE RUB;

I LOSE A THOUSAND AT THE BEST,
THEN GET THE GIRLS TO TAKE THE REST!

I GO OFF TO MAXIM'S
WHERE FUN AND FROLIC BEAMS!

WITH ALL THE GIRLS I CHATTER,
I LAUGH AND KISS AND FLATTER!

LOLO, DODO, JOU-JOU,
CLO-CLO, MARGOT, FROU-FROU,

FOR SURNAMES DO NOT MATTER
I TAKE THE FIRST TO HAND!

AND THEN THE CORKS GO POP!
WE DANCE AND NEVER STOP!

THE LADIES SMILE SO SWEETLY,
I CATCH AND KISS THEM NEATLY!

LOLO, DODO, JOU-JOU,
CLO-CLO, MARGOT, FROU-FROU

TILL I FORGET COMPLETELY
 MY DEAR OLD FATHERLAND!

I'M HAPPY AT MAXIM'S
 WHERE FUN AND FROLIC BEAMS!

WITH ALL THE GIRLS I CHATTER,
 I LAUGH AND KISS AND FLATTER!

LOLO, DODO, JOU-JOU,
 CLO-CLO, MARGOT, FROU-FROU,

FOR SURNAMES DO NOT MATTER
 I TAKE THE FIRST TO HAND!

AND THEN THE CORKS GO POP!
 WE DANCE AND NEVER STOP!

THE LADIES SMILE SO SWEETLY,
 I CATCH AND KISS THEM NEATLY!

LOLO, DODO, JOU-JOU,
 CLO-CLO, MARGOT, FROU-FROU

TILL I FORGET COMPLETELY
 MY DEAR OLD FATHERLAND!

THEN I REFRESH MY JADED BRAIN
 WITH LITTLE SUPPERS AND CHAMPAGNE.

AND LOOK INTO THE LADIES' EYES
 TILL THEY AND I ARE CLOSE ALLIES!

SO IN A GLASS OF GOLDEN WINE,
 AN ENTENTE CORDIAL I SIGN;

FOR I CAN DO THAT SORT OF THING
 AS WELL AS ANY OTHER KING!

THEN I ALLOW THE LOVELY SEX
TO WEAR MY ARMS AROUND THEIR NECKS,

AND GIVE THE WAITER AT THE DOOR
AN ORDER FOR A DOZEN MORE!

I'M HAPPY AT MAXIM'S
WHERE FUN AND FROLIC BEAMS!

WITH ALL THE GIRLS I CHATTER,
I LAUGH AND KISS AND FLATTER!

LOLO, DODO, JOU-JOU,
CLO-CLO, MARGOT, FROU-FROU,

FOR SURNAMES DO NOT MATTER
I TAKE THE FIRST TO HAND!

AND THEN THE CORKS GO POP!
WE DANCE AND NEVER STOP!

THE LADIES SMILE SO SWEETLY,
I CATCH AND KISS THEM NEATLY!

LOLO, DODO, JOU-JOU,
CLO-CLO, MARGOT, FROU-FROU

TILL I FORGET COMPLETELY
MY DEAR OLD FATHERLAND!

MUSIC transitions to a waltz.

*The SS GUARDS rise from their positions and join
HANSEL in a chorus line. They ALL sing
(to the tune of **"THE MERRY WIDOW WALTZ"**):*

BUREAUCRAT OF THE REALM
HE'S SO FAMOUS!

GUARD 1

WHO CAN BLAME US?

GUARD 2

WE'RE SO PROUD!

ALL GUARDS

HE'S OUR IDOL!
HENCE HIS TITLE:
"GOD-EN-DOWED!"

GUARD 3

EV'RY ONE ADORES HIM!

BUREAUCRAT OF THE REALM

EV'RY ONE AGREES!

ALL GUARDS

THE FATHERLAND
SHOULD BOW TO HIM
ON BEN-DED KNEES!

> *ALL break into a dance, the SS GUARDS taking turns waltzing with HANSEL as ALL vocalize in harmony to the tune:*

ALL

LAH-LA, LAH-LA
LAH-LA, LAH-LA
LAAH, LAAH, LAAH!

LAH-LA, LAH-LA
LAH-LA, LAH-LA
LAAH, LAAH, LAAH!

LAH-LA, LAH-LA
LAH, LA-LAH,
LAH-LA, LAH, LA-LAAH!

LAH-LA, LAH-LA
LAH-LA-LAH,
LA-LAH, LAAH, LAAH!

GUARD 1

GIVE US CIRCUS!

GUARD 2

GIVE US BREAD!

BUREAUCRAT OF THE REALM
AND FAVORS—JUST A FEW!

ALL
THEN WE'LL GO WHERE WE ARE LED!

HANSEL and ALL GUARDS
(Big finish:)
YOU—WOULD—TOOOOOOO!

*LIGHTS narrow down to HANSEL as the GUARDS exit.
HANSEL takes his bows as
the MUSIC fades away.*

HANSEL

Danke, danke, danke...

Scene 6

*LIGHTS come up on the dressing room area. HANSEL,
wiping sweat from his brow, grabs the microphone and
speaks:*

LAUTSPRECHER

Hansel Hals Returns To His Dressing Room As The Play Approaches Its Final Scene. Soon, Soon, His Night's Work Will Be Done...

> *Applause is heard on the monitor, giving way to snatches of dialogue, as HANSEL enters the dressing room. HE is old. Old. 100 years old. He sits heavily in his chair. Exhausted, he wipes his brow, checks his makeup, listens to the monitor. GERHART and OSCAR (played by the actor who played FRANZ and is playing GAEV in "The Cherry Orchard") enter the dressing room.*

GERHART

Went well for you out there?

HANSEL

Better. Yes. Thank you...

OSCAR/FRANZ

More comfortable?

HANSEL

Yes. Got a few laughs.

GERHART

Ha! You see?

> *GERHART checks his cell phone for messages...*

OSCAR/FRANZ

BIG laughs! You killed 'em!

HANSEL

Yes.

GERHART

And you've still got it, old man!

OSCAR/FRANZ

Sure have! Hope I can keep it going like you!

HANSEL

Well—
     (Laughs)
I am the old circus elephant! You know that story? The circus
elephant...?

OSCAR/FRANZ

Which...?

HANSEL

The old circus elephant is about go out to the ring for the first
performance of the day. His handler wishes to keep the pooping
to a minimum, you see?—so he takes a long-handled brush,
rinses it out, shoves it deep into the elephant's—you know—and
starts to clean it out.
     (Demonstrates the action...)
The old elephant turns his head around to face the handler and
he says: "How's the house?"

GERHART and OSCAR/FRANZ laugh.

HANSEL (cont'd)

So, that's me! The old circus elephant! Clean me out and point
me toward the stage! I'm ready! "Where's the stage and what
are we playing?!" I'm a war horse!

OSCAR/FRANZ

Old Trouper!

HANSEL

Nothing stops me!

GERHART

Nothing!

HANSEL

Except, maybe, an angry mob and a blitzkrieg of rotten tomatoes!

> *There is a pause. OSCAR and GERHART laugh uncomfortably...*

HANSEL (cont'd)

Oh, boy!

> *There is another pause. Nervous laughter from OSCAR and GERHART. Snippets of muffled dialogue from "The Cherry Orchard" are heard over the monitor...*

HANSEL (cont'd)

That was really something!

OSCAR/FRANZ

I can't imagine...

GERHART

No. It must have been...

HANSEL

"The Sound Of Music"—? No! The Sound Of Disaster! *Boom!* I bombed in Amsterdam!

> *OSCAR and GERHART laugh.*

HANSEL (cont'd)

And Amsterdam bombed me—with rotten vegetables! They came armed!

OSCAR and GERHART laugh.

HANSEL (cont'd)

What a Homecoming! What an Opening Night! Idiot producers...

> *HE stands up. With exaggerated drama, HE quotes a few lines as Captain von Trapp from "The Sound Of Music"*

HANSEL (cont'd)

"Children, the Nazis have offered me, Captain Georg Ludwig Ritter von Trapp, a commission. I'm to report to the naval base at Bremerhaven. To refuse the Nazis would be fatal—to all of us. To JOIN the Nazis: UNTHINKABLE!"

> *There is another pause. Snippets of muffled dialogue from "The Cherry Orchard" are heard over the monitor...*

HANSEL (cont'd)

...Then the vegetables fly! The stage becomes like a farmers' market in two seconds! Then they actually stormed the stage! Chased me into the wings! I hid in the ladies' dressing room and locked the door!

OSCAR and GERHART laugh.

HANSEL (cont'd)

Show over! Curtain! They didn't even let me sing "Edelweiss"!

OSCAR and GERHART laugh.

HANSEL (cont'd)
And, believe me, I can sing the crap out of "Edelweiss!"

OSCAR and GERHART laugh loudly.

HANSEL (cont'd)
(Loosely paraphrasing Captain von Trapp:)
"Children, as you know, I hate the Nazis! Nazis stink! Like poop!—"
    (Sings:)
"EDELWEISS, EDELWEISS—"

OSCAR and GERHART laugh loudly. SILKE (as the actor who plays LUBOV in "The Cherry Orchard") pops her head into the dressing room.

LUBOV/SILKE
Quiet! Quiet! They can hear you on stage!

LUBOV/SILKE withdraws. The MEN shut up, then resume speaking in normal tones...

GERHART
That must have been horrible.

HANSEL
Yes. It gave me a heavy heart. Unwelcome in my native Homeland. Because of a little favor I did in a time of war. Unforgiven. Not even one full performance! Everybody unemployed. Tossed into the gutter...

OSCAR/FRANZ
It wasn't your fault, though... I mean—

HANSEL
Yes! Idiot producers! Too soon. For me? In that role? It was twenty years after the war, but, still...

There is a pause. Snippets of muffled dialogue from "The Cherry Orchard" are heard over the monitor...

HANSEL (cont'd)
Oh, but I was perfect for the role. Perfect. I understand Captain von Trapp...

GERHART
Mm-hmm.

OSCAR/FRANZ
Uh-huh.

HANSEL
He doesn't compromise. Demands perfection. Values loyalty. Sings beautifully...

HANSEL laughs. OSCAR and GERHART chuckle a little.

HANSEL (cont'd)
Von Trapp—He doesn't follow the easy path. No. He always does what his conscience dictates. Even if it means danger. I understand that. Like von Trapp, I lived that!

OSCAR/FRANZ
(Simultaneous with GERHART)
But he escapes—

GERHART
(Simultaneous with OSCAR/FRANZ)
The family leaves the—

There is a pause. Snippets of muffled dialogue from "The Cherry Orchard" are heard over the Monitor...

OSCAR/FRANZ
But, don't they escape the Nazis? In "The Sound Of Music?"

HANSEL
Yes. Of course.

GERHART
Over the Alps...?

HANSEL
Yes.

OSCAR/FRANZ
Go into exile...?

HANSEL
Exile... Yes...

GERHART
But you … stayed.

There is a pause.

SOUND from the monitor ceases.

*LIGHTS begin to faintly illuminate a playing area
where "The Cherry Orchard" is being performed. The
actor playing SILKE enters this playing area in her role
as LUBOV/SILKE. SHE takes a seated position on a
sofa and holds it. Also entering this playing area is the
actor who plays FRIKA, now taking the role of ANYA/
FRIKA in this final scene of "The Cherry Orchard."
SHE also takes a seated position on the sofa and
holds it, as HANSEL, looking all of his 100 years or
so, continues to speak. OSCAR and GERHART listen,
fascinated...*

HANSEL

I stayed. Yes. I didn't leave, like all those others. And what did I do wrong? Sure, I acted in films for the Third Reich. Entertainment films. Sure, I wanted to make my career. Why should I not? I saw my good, proud, Dutch name on half the movie posters in the Realm! But my friends, in Berlin?—they left me. Alone. Exiled. Friends? Ha. I had no friends. Only fans. And they loved me. Gave me reason to go on living. And I loved them. How could I abandon them? I couldn't! So: What did I do wrong? Nothing. The Allies agreed, after the war. They allowed me to continue to work. For my admirers... Oh, I had so many admirers. If von Trapp had admirers, as many admirers as I had, well... I was ordered to Dachau! To refuse would have been fatal! Von Trapp, yes, he was ordered to Bremerhaven, but that was the early years of the Reich! The Thirties! It was easier then. One could flee, they say... But when I was ordered to Dachau, the Reich was established! A machine! It was the Forties! It wouldn't have been so easy for von Trapp in the Forties! *"So long/ Farewell/Auf wiedersehen/ Good night—?"* Phooey! Not so easy! Not in the Forties. And I was *Gottbegnadeter.* Endowed. By *God.* I was a National Treasure, for God's sake! Me, a Dutchman, a German National Treasure! And I knew my duty. I remained. I *worked!*

A disembodied VOICE, as the Stage Manager, booms over the monitor:

LAUTSPRECHER
Lopakhin! Gaev! To the stage! You missed your cue!

OSCAR/FRANZ
(Simultaneous with GERHART.)
Shit!

GERHART
(Simultaneous with OSCAR/FRANZ.)
Fuck me dead!

*OSCAR and GERHART leap to their feet and bolt from
the dressing room. The LAUTSPRECHER booms again:*

LAUTSPRECHER (cont'd)
Lopakhin! Gaev! To the stage!

*HANSEL watches OSCAR and GERHART as they flee,
but continues speaking...*

HANSEL
They left me behind... Exiled me... I did what I could... For
the people... Gave everything... Bled myself dry... For my art...
Gottbegnadeter... We were artists...! Ordered to Dachau... It was
a great show, too... A triumph... I *killed*...!

Scene 7

*LIGHTS come up full on the "Cherry Orchard" playing
area. LUBOV/SILKE and ANYA/FRIKA stand and
begin dialogue as LIGHTS grow faint on HANSEL in the
dressing room.*

LUBOV/SILKE
(Looks around the house)
Goodbye, dear house! The winter will go, the spring will come,
and then you'll exist no more. The orchard will be chopped
down and you will be pulled down. Oh, how much these walls
have seen!

ANYA/FRIKA
A new life is beginning, mother!...

*There is a long, expectant pause. Then LUBOV/SILKE
repeats an improvised version of her last line. ANYA/*

FRIKA will do the same, as they are both trying to cover
for the missed entrances of GAEV and LOPAKHIN...

LUBOV/SILKE
... How much, yes, how very much, these walls have seen... And the orchard will be chopped down... Chopped down...

ANYA/FRIKA
...Yes, mother. Yes. A new life is beginning... A new... A brand new life is beginning ... mother...

Another expectant pause...

LUBOV/SILKE
... Goodbye—walls...

ANYA/FRIKA
Goodbye—doors... And here's to a new life ._ a brand ... *a brand new life! ... which is beginning! ... mother!...*

LOPAKHIN/GERHART and GAEV/FRANZ, both
noticeably panicked and out of breath, but trying to
conceal their distress at being late for their cue, burst onto
the playing area.

GAEV/FRANZ
Yes! Everything's all right now!

LOPAKHIN/GERHART
Yes! Now that the question is solved once and for all!

GAEV/FRANZ
Yes! Everything's all right!—Before the orchard was sold—red down the middle—we were all upset!

LOPAKHIN/GERHART

But now we are all calm!

GAEV/FRANZ

All calm! And you, Luba, you look better! There's no doubt about that!

LUBOV/SILKE

And now we can leave. But I have anxieties still. First, poor Firs: Has Firs been sent to the hospital?
(Looks at her watch)
We still have a few minutes.

ANYA/FRIKA

I gave orders this morning, mother. I suppose they have sent him.

LUBOV/SILKE

(To GAEV)
Leonid Andreyevitch, have we time to make inquiries if Firs has been sent to the hospital?

LOPAKHIN/GERHART

The aged Firs, in my opinion, is hardly worth the mending! But Yasha sent him off to the hospital this morning. They will send the doctor's letter after him.

LUBOV/SILKE

Well, then. That is settled. Now we can go away...

ANYA/FRIKA

Away!

GAEV/FRANZ

My friends! My dear friends! Can I be silent in leaving this house forever more? Can I restrain myself, in saying farewell, from expressing my deepest, most heartfelt—

ANYA/FRIKA

Uncle! Please!

LUBOV/SILKE

Brother...

GAEV/FRANZ

(Stupidly)
Double the red, into the middle... I'll be quiet.

LOPAKHIN/GERHART

Well, it's time to be off. Before the woodsmen take to their axes...

LUBOV/SILKE

And Firs...?

ANYA/FRIKA

At the hospital, mother! As we have said! Don't worry!

LUBOV/SILKE

Then... we must go.

ANYA/FRIKA

Goodbye, home! Goodbye, old life!

LOPAKHIN/GERHART

Welcome, new life! Eh?

*LOPAKHIN/GERHART escorts ANYA/FRIKA to the
door. HANSEL is seen rising from his place in the faintly-
lit dressing room. HE adjusts his costume, leaves the
dressing room, and the lights on that area go out...*

LOPAKHIN/GERHART (cont'd)

Till the spring, then! Come on... Till we meet again!

LOPAKHIN/GERHART and ANYA/FRIKA exit.
LUBOV/SILKE and GAEV/FRANZ, left alone, fall into
each other's arms. They weep, restrainedly and quietly...

GAEV/FRANZ
(In despair)
My sister, my sister...

ANYA/FRIKA
(Calling, offstage)
Mother!

LOPAKHIN/GERHART
(Calling, offstage)
Coo-eee!

LUBOV/SILKE
To look at the walls and the windows for the last time... My
dead mother used to like to walk about this room...

GAEV/FRANZ
My sister, my sister!

ANYA/FRIKA
(Calling, offstage)
Mother!

LOPAKHIN/GERHART
(Calling, offstage)
Coo-eee!

LUBOV/SILKE
We're coming!

THEY go out, close the door. The sound of keys locking
the door is heard, then the sound of a carriage going

away. It is quiet. Then the sound of an axe hitting a tree repeatedly is heard.

FIRS/HANSEL enters. He is ill. Feeble. Old. Very, very old. He goes to the door and tries the handle.

FIRS/HANSEL

It's locked. They've gone away.
(Sits on the sofa)
They've forgotten about me. Never mind, I'll sit here... And Leonid Andreyevitch will have gone in a light overcoat instead of putting on his fur coat, I suppose...
(Sighs anxiously)
I didn't see... Oh, these young people!
(Mumbles something that cannot be understood)
Life's gone on as if I'd never lived.
(Lying down)
I'll lie down... Ach, you've no strength left in you, nothing left at all... Oh, you ... bungler!

HANSEL lies without moving, closes his eyes as if falling asleep. The sound of the axe falling on a tree continues. And another, distant, sound is heard, as if from the sky, of a breaking string, dying away sadly. LIGHTS begin to fade. Gradually, voices begin to be heard from the monitor—a shout: "Boo!" More shouts, hoots, "Boo, Boooo!" "Fascist!" "Collaborator!" HANSEL opens his eyes. Apprehensive, HE half-rises from the sofa, looks out at the audience. The shouts grow louder and louder, more and more angry. "Fascist!" "Irredeemable!" "Collaborator!" Then:

BLACKOUT

END OF PLAY

*Production Notes

—All of the music and lyrics of "The Merry Widow" used in this play are from the original English translation published in 1907. Both the music and translated lyrics are in the Public Domain. The complete score of "The Merry Widow" for piano and voice is available from Dover Publications, Inc., New York, as an unabridged reprint of the 1907 original.

—Sheet music and lyrics for the German traditional songs used in this play, as well as the music and lyrics original with the playwright, are in the Appendix.

—All other music indicated in the script is at the discretion of the producer and director.

—Questions? Please contact the playwright through his website: www.billdam.com

Appendix

Traditional and original music

"SUSE LEWE SUSE" page 128

"THE WATCH ON THE RHINE" page 129

"NOTHING AT ALL" page 130

"NEUTRAL MAN" page 133

SUSE LEWE SUSE
German Folk Song

Traditional

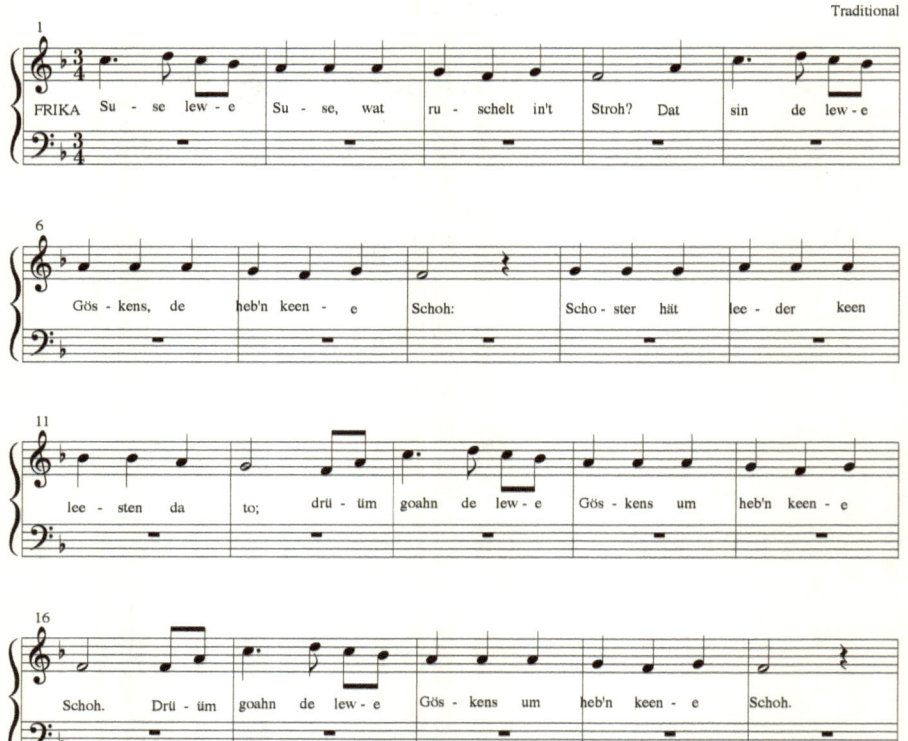

FRIKA Su - se lewe - e Su - se, wat ru - schelt in't Stroh? Dat sin de lew - e Gös - kens, de heb'n keen - e Schoh: Scho - ster hät lee - der keen lee - sten da to; drü - üm goahn de lew - e Gös - kens um heb'n keen - e Schoh. Drü - üm goahn de lew - e Gös - kens um heb'n keen - e Schoh.

1

THE WATCH ON THE RHINE

Frika

Public Domain

The cry re - sounds like thun - der's peal, like crash - ing waves

and clang of steel: the Rhine, the Rhine, our Ger - man Rhine,

who will de - fend our stream di - vine? Dear Fa - ther land,

no fear be thine, Lieb' Va - ter - land, magst ru - hig sein,

firm and true stands the watch, the watch on

the Rhine! Fest steht und treu die Wacht,

die Wacht am Rhein!

1

NOTHING AT ALL
Hansel

William Damkoehler

Hansel

To - day we are lov - ers, to -

PIANO

mor - row we're strang - ers. Yes - ter - day's dreams sweet

1

130

Fate re - ar - rang - es. So, stop up my

tears; oh, wait -- I have none. They fled with all those

oth - ers who have left me, a - ban - doned. One

* Ped.   * Ped.   * Ped.   * Ped.

2

NEUTRAL MAN
Silke

William Damkoehler

SILKE

He's NEU-TRAL MAN, Has no af-fi-li-a-tion. Does what he can for his wear-y na-tion. He sees all

PIANO

1

sides of all si - tu - a - tions. Does what he must to main - tain good re-

la - tions. And when it comes to ma - king choi - ces, he gives the

floor to the loud - est voi - ces. (Spoken: Is that any way to act? I ask you.)

He thinks the world could ne-ver wors-en If he sees good in ev'-ry per-son. And when they cheer, and pay him fa-vor, that's all he asks: this sim-ple gift to sa-vor. For he

3

136

He thinks the rule: "Do un - to, and be done by", the nobl - est
code of liv - ing to be come by... Now comes the shock when he dis -
cov - ers that his be - liefs are not shared by oth - ers.

Ped. *Ped. Ped. * Ped. *

Ped. Ped. *Ped. *

Ped. *Ped. * Ped.

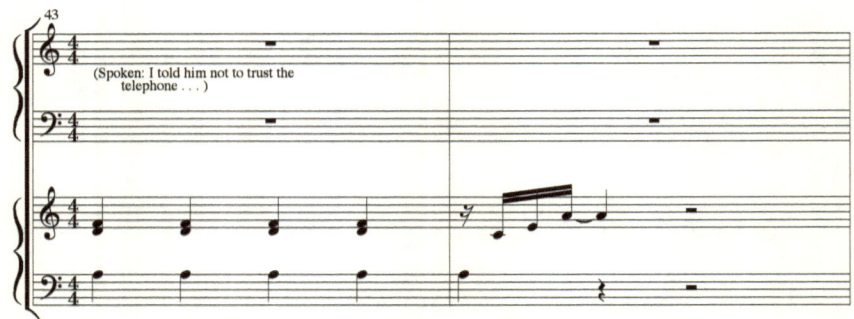

(Spoken: I told him not to trust the
telephone . . .)

Ped.

6

Acknowledgements

I wish to thank, foremost, my bawdy American poet friend Fred Rosenblum for his support and advocacy for my work, without which the publication of this volume would not have happened. Thank you, Fred.

I gratefully acknowledge, too, Curt Columbus of Trinity Repertory Company and Tyler Dobrowsky of Philadelphia Theatre Company for encouraging me as an "emerging" playwright! Your generous gifts of your time and insight have helped me immeasurably.

Furthermore, to the administrative staff and the artists of Trinity Repertory Company who have been my colleagues over the years and who contributed to the success of my play workshops — my deepest thanks.

And integral to the development of my plays are Esteban Alvarado and the insanely talented writers in Esteban's Writers Workshop at San Diego College of Continuing Education. Thanks, all, for your enthusiastic support!

Thank you, Donna Bister, for your diligent and meticulous management of Fomite's production process.

And finally, profound gratitude to the late Marc Estrin, who, along with Donna Bister, established Fomite Press in 2011, giving a publishing home to hundreds of poets, novelists, playwrights, and "odd birds," myself included. Marc's sharp editorial mind and his nurturing nature significantly improved my work; and I have no doubt my sentiment is shared by everyone fortunate enough to have collaborated with this remarkable "modern Renaissance Man." Thank you, Marc.

About the Author

In a career spanning four decades as a member of the renowned Trinity Repertory Company's resident acting ensemble, William Damkoehler appeared in well over a hundred productions, either in Trinity's home spaces in Providence, RI, or with the company on Broadway, at the Edinburgh Theatre Festival in Scotland, in Boston, in Philadelphia, or on the venerable Straw Hat Summer Theater Circuit. Favorite roles include Ebenezer Scrooge, Macheath, George Antrobus and James Tyrone in *A Christmas Carol, The Threepenny Opera, The Skin Of Our Teeth,* and *Long Day's Journey Into Night,* respectively. At Trinity, William also served as Director or Musical Director for many main-stage productions.

As a Theater Educator, William held for many years the position of Senior Lecturer at Rhode Island School Of Design where he established an ongoing Acting and Theater Production elective program in the Liberal Arts Division. He created and directed a touring group of senior citizens who performed "kitchen band" music and wrote and performed their own short comedies around the state in the Cranston, RI chapter of RSVP, the original federal Retired Senior Volunteer Program. He also taught and directed at Rhode Island College.

In addition to his playwriting, William's free-lance writing saw non-fiction articles published in *The Providence Journal-Bulletin* and *The New York Times*. Excerpts of other fiction appear in the anthologies "For The Love Of Writing" and "The Stories Start Here".

William currently lives in San Diego, California with his wife, Cynthia Strickland — also retired from Trinity Rep's acting ensemble.

Fomite

Writing a review on social media sites for readers will help the progress of independent publishing. To submit a review, go to the book page on any of the sites and follow the links for reviews. Books from independent presses rely on reader-to-reader communications.

For more information or to order any of our books, visit:
fomitepress.com/our-books.html

More plays and theater pieces from Fomite...

William Damkoehler — *The Occupant and Self-Storage*

Stephen Goldberg — *Screwed and Other Plays*

Vincenzo Lamartora/Michael Palma — *The Dimension of Loss*

Michele Markarian — *Unborn Children of America*

Hanna Eady and Edward Mast — *The Mulberry Tree and The Return*

David Schein — *My Murder and Other Local News*

David Schein — *Stones: (a deconstruction of Zion)*

David Schein — *Tokens: A Play on the Plague*